Carol Vorderman's Guide to the Internet

You honestly don't need a degree in astrophysics to enjoy the Internet, and you'll hardly even use your keyboard – just your mouse to point your cursor and then click. Once you've learned what to click and when to click (it's simple, trust me), nothing less than a whole new world of learning, information and experience will open up in front of you.

The Internet has begun to change the way that many of us work and play. Before long it will also change the way our children are educated – and that's one of the main reasons why I wanted to get involved with this book.

I started using the Internet in 1995 but to be honest I found it quite slow, very technical and not that visually interesting. How things have changed in that short time! Three years on and I'm hooked and what's more so is my 70-year-old mother – once you start on the Internet it is fantastic.

This book helps you to understand how the Internet works and what you can find on it; it will also help you to control your children's access in a way that still leaves room for them to explore freely.

I consider myself privileged to be associated with Rob Young, who has written a number of computer books. In fact, it was one of Rob's books that taught me a whole lot about the Internet. Thanks Rob. He has spent a lot of time finding some of the most weird and wonderful sites, so we both hope that you enjoy this book and that it helps you to enter the truly inspirational world of the Internet.

OK, it's time to get started. Turn the page, switch on your computer and get ready for the world's greatest encyclopaedia and meeting room – updated every second of the day.

Enjoy!

Carol Vorderman's Guide to the Internet

by Carol Vorderman & Rob Young

Prentice Hall Europe

London New York Toronto Sydney Tokyo Singapore
Madrid Mexico City Munich Paris

First published 1998 by
Prentice Hall Europe
Campus 400, Maylands Avenue
Hemel Hempstead
Hertfordshire, HP2 7EZ
A division of Simon & Schuster International Group

Editorial, design and typesetting by
Brown Packaging Books Ltd,
Bradley's Close, 74–77 White Lion Street, London N1 9PF

Printed and bound in Great Britain by
TJ International, Padstow, Cornwall

British Library Cataloguing in Publication Data

A catalogue record for this book is available from the
British Library

Library of Congress Cataloging-in-Publication Data

A catalogue record for this book is available from
the Library of Congress

ISBN 0-13-079983-1

3 4 5   02 01 00 99

Also by Rob Young:

The Midi Files

The Windows 95 Black Box

The UK Internet Starter Kit

The *What PC?* Guide to your PC

Licensing Agreement

This book comes with a CD software package. By opening this package, you are agreeing to be bound by the following:

pension

Moneywise Guide to Your Pension

Whatever your age or income, this book will help you to decide on the right pension for a comfortable retirement, free from constant worries about money.

£8.99 ISBN: 0-13-911066-6

planning your finances

Moneywise Guide to Planning Your Finances

Inside you'll find lots of tips on how to make your money go that much further, plus sound advice on getting the best deals on savings, mortgages and tax.

£8.99 ISBN: 0-13-911041-0

Moneywise Guide to Investing in the Stockmarket

However much money you have to invest, and whatever your attitude to risk, this book will help you make the right stockmarket choices every time.

£8.99 ISBN: 0-13-911033-X

tax

Moneywise Guide to Tax

Addressing basic questions, with tax saving tips plus a step-by-step guide to Self Assessment and tax returns, this book is an essential guide, whatever your circumstances.

£8.99 ISBN: 0-13-911058-5

Moneywise is the UK's best-selling consumer finance magazine. Since its launch in 1990 it has won numerous awards, including Consumer Finance Magazine of the Year 1996 in the Bradford & Bingley journalism awards and Consumer Publication of the Year 1996 in the personal finance Golden Pen Awards. It covers every aspect of personal finance from insurance to investment and PEPs to pensions. It runs a free advice service and responds to all readers' letters.

investing in the stockmarket

THE MONEYWISE GUIDES ARE AVAILABLE FROM WH SMITH AND OTHER GOOD BOOKSTORES

Contents

Contents

Chapter 7:
Newsgroup Discussions & Debates

Chapter 8:
Chat & Talk – Live Conversations

Contents

Contents

Contents

Introduction

The Internet really hit the headlines in 1994. People started talking about it, newspapers started writing articles about it and those strange-looking addresses full of dots and dashes started popping up at the end of TV shows and adverts.

Ah yes, everyone said, knowingly. Hype. It'll be something different next year. But something unexpected happened.

Unlike most other objects of media hype in recent years, after the dust has settled, millions of people are still using the Internet every day – for entertainment, for business, for leisure, to communicate with others, to learn or research – the list is almost endless. And every day the number of people using the Internet grows by thousands. If these people weren't finding it useful, or enjoyable, that number would be getting smaller instead.

These people can't all be computing experts either, can they? In fact, you don't have to be a technical genius to use the Internet. As long as you're reasonably comfortable with using a PC and Windows, it's no more tricky than anything else you use your computer for. That's the thing that really happened in 1994: although the Internet has been around since the 1960s, software suddenly started to appear that made it friendly and easy to use.

But that's history, and we're not going to bore you with history lessons, or throw a lot of impressive but unnecessary jargon at you. The aim of this book is twofold – first, to help you connect your computer to the Internet and find your way around it, and second, to point you towards the practical, useful or enjoyable things that the Internet has to offer. To that end, any technical detail that you won't need straight away has been banished to the Glossary at the back of the book.

Why do you need a UK guide to the Internet?

In the UK we use the Internet differently from our American counterparts: different companies provide the services we need, charge different prices for them and give us different options to choose from. And once we're connected, we want to find the information that matters to us, so we need to look in different places to find it. In addition, because we're not American (or French, or Italian...), our interests, habits, laws, environment and whole way of life differ enormously. These affect both the way we use the Internet, and what we use it for.

▷ Most American users have access to free local phone calls, which means that they can stay connected to the Internet all day long for no extra charge. In the UK, where we still pay by the minute, to follow some of the suggestions given in an American guide could end up costing a small fortune! Throughout this book, it's assumed that you want your time on the Internet to have as little impact as possible on the size of your phone bill.

▷ As a UK user, you want to find UK information. For example, you want to read UK newspapers and

magazines; see local weather forecasts; check local
TV listings and sports results; find out what's
showing at your nearest cinema; use UK travel
agents, hotels, airlines and trains; plan days out at
UK theme parks and museums and so on.

▷ Many Internet sites give support, help and advice
on any subject you can imagine. Although some
American Internet books can point you towards
valuable information, they won't tell you where to
get the best UK legal or consumer advice, find a job
or discuss financial matters with other UK
investors.

Icons & conventions

Throughout the book you'll see a few special features
and conventions that make it easier to find your way
around. In particular you'll notice that chapters are
split up into bite-sized chunks with subheadings. You'll
also find some icons and text in boxes containing
extra information that you might find useful or
interesting:

A question-and-answer format highlighting
questions or problems that might present
themselves while you're reading about
something or trying it out yourself.

Provides handy hints, tips and incidental
notes that might save you some time, point
you in a new direction or help you to
avoid pitfalls.

Explains any technical terms that couldn't
be avoided, or any related jargon that you
might encounter when dealing with a
particular area of the Internet.

We've also used different type-styles and keyboard
conventions to make particular meanings clear, as
shown in the table on the next page.

Introduction

Convention	Description
bold type	Indicates a new term being encountered, an Internet address or text that you'll type yourself.
bold-italic type	Sometimes what you have to type will depend on what you're trying to do. In those cases, bold-italics are used to indicate that you'll replace this text with your own. For example, if you have to type the name of a file you want to open, you'll see something like **open** *filename*.
Ctrl + C	A key-combination, saving frequent mouse excursions to pull down menus. The keys to press will be separated by **+** signs. This example means press and hold the **Ctrl** key while pressing **C** once.
File | Open	Means that you should open the software's **File** menu, and select its **Open** option. You might see something longer, such as View | Options | General: in this case you'll open the **View** menu, select the **Options** entry and then click on something that says **General** – it may be a button or a tabbed page, but it will always be obvious when you get there!
Directories	To users of Windows 95 and later, these are better known as **folders**. On the Internet (as in MS-DOS and Windows 3.1) they're known as **directories**, but the meaning is the same.

Introducing the Internet

In This Chapter...

⇨ Find out what the Internet really is

⇨ Discover some of the great things you can do on the Net

⇨ Meet the six most popular areas of the Internet

⇨ What do you need, and what does it cost?

Before you can really get excited at the prospect of 'getting on the Internet', it helps to have some idea of what it really is, what you can use it for and how it works.

So let's start by looking at how the Internet is organised, and at some of the ways you can use it. We'll also introduce most of the technical detail you'll need to know in this chapter. It's all quite painless, though, and hopefully this appetiser will leave you hungry for the main course.

What is the Internet?

This is the obvious first question, but let's try and skip through its literal answer as fast as possible. The technical explanation is that it's a giant, world-wide computer network made up of lots of smaller computer networks. As with any network, these computers are connected to one another so that they can share information. Unlike most networks, though, the vastness of the Internet means that this information has to be passed around using modems and telephone lines rather than an office full of cables.

But all that's just hardware, and it's probably not making your mouth water. Instead, let's zoom in on that word 'information', the key to the real Internet. The types of information these computers can share cover a huge (and expanding) range – pictures, sounds, text, video, applications, music and much more – making the Internet a true multimedia experience. Anyone can connect their computer to the Internet and gain instant access to millions of files.

How big is the Internet?

When it comes to numbers, no-one knows. A lot of informed guess-work goes on, but it doesn't look terribly well informed when you compare results. It's safest just to say that millions of computers are serving tens of millions of people and leave it at that.

People power

The other aspect of the real Internet is people. All the information you'll find is put there by real people, often simply because they want to share their knowledge, skills, interests or creations with anyone who's interested. The people themselves may be companies keen to promote their products; organisations such as universities, charities and governments; or individual users like you and me.

Along with people, of course, comes communication, and the Internet is a powerful communications system. You can exchange messages (email) with other users, hold conversations or online meetings by typing messages back and forth or by actually sending your voice over the Internet using a microphone instead of a telephone, and take part in any of 28,000 discussion groups covering more subjects than you can imagine.

In addition, the Internet can be immensely useful, or just plain fun — you can browse around, or search for some specific item. As a taste:

▷ Control robots and movie cameras on other continents while the live camera footage is beamed straight to your desktop.

▷ Book a skiing holiday online and check the snow conditions in your chosen resort with up-to-the-minute pictures.

▷ Explore 3-dimensional 'virtual reality' worlds and play games with people visiting the same world.

▷ Learn about any subject under the sun, research projects with text, sound, pictures and video or get in touch with the experts.

▷ Download the latest versions and updates of your software long before they hit the shops or be among the first to use brand new 'test editions' of major software titles (known as beta releases).

Download

The act of copying a file from one distant computer across a network of computers and telephone lines to your own hard disk. The opposite term is 'upload' – copying a file from your own disk to a remote computer.

The popular Internet services

What you've just read is a general taste of what's on offer on the Net, but all the things you want to do (or get or see) will be scattered around the world on different computers. In other words, these computers offer the services you want to use. The Internet is made up of a bundle of different services, but here's a quick look at the five most popular:

▷ **Email.** Email is the oldest and most used of the Internet services with millions of messages whizzing around it every day. Most email messages are just ordinary text, but you can attach almost any type of computer file you want to send along with it (such as a spreadsheet or a small program), and encrypt the message so that no-one except the intended recipient will be able to read it.

▷ **The World Wide Web.** This service, often known simply as the Web, has had so much publicity and acclaim that you might think it *is* the Internet. In fact, it's the Net's new baby, born in 1992. It's a very lively, gurgling baby though, packed with pictures, text, video, music and information on almost any subject you care to think of. All the pages on the Web are linked together, so that a page you're viewing from a computer in Bristol might lead you to a page in Tokyo, Brisbane or Oslo with a single mouse-click. Many individual users have their own pages on the Web, along with multinational companies, political parties, universities and colleges, football teams, local councils, and so on, and so on.

▷ **Newsgroups.** A newsgroup is a discussion group that focuses on one particular subject. The discussion itself takes place through a form of email, but the big difference is that these messages are posted for the whole group to read and respond to. You can join any group you like from a choice of over 28,000, with subjects ranging from spina-bifida support to alien landings, James Bond films and Turkish culture.

▷ **Chat.** This isn't chat as in 'yakety-yak', more 'clickety-click'. You can hold conversations with one or more people by typing messages back and forth which instantly appear on the screens of everyone involved. Some recent chat programs allow 'whiteboarding' (drawing pictures and diagrams in collaboration), private online conferences and control of programs running on someone else's computer.

▷ **Voice on the Net.** This *is* chat as in 'yakety-yak'. As long as you've got a soundcard in your computer, and a microphone plugged into it, you can talk to anyone in the world just as you do with the telephone (provided they're online and have a soundcard and microphone too). So why not use the telephone? Your Internet connection will be a local call, letting you hold these conversations for as little as 60p per hour. Compare that with the cost of a direct-dialled call to New York (roughly £14.40 per hour) and you've got a pretty good reason!

Although other services exist, these are almost certainly the ones you'll be using most (and you may use nothing but email and the World Wide Web – the services are there if you want them, but you don't have to use them).

Understanding Internet addresses

So the Internet is big, the computers that form the Internet are counted in millions, and yet somehow all that information manages to get wherever it's supposed to go. But how does that tiny, helpless file find its way from deepest Ohio to your own computer all by itself?

In much the same way that an ordinary letter manages to arrive at your house: it has an address attached to it that identifies one single house in the whole world. Every single computer on the Internet has a unique address, called its **IP address**, which consists of four numbers separated by dots, such as 194.72.6.226.

IP address

'IP' stands for Internet Protocol. IP works with its best friend, TCP, to handle the tricky job of sending computer files down telephone lines, and part of this job is knowing which computer is asking for the file and which is sending it.

Domain names – the easier way

Of course, if you need to connect to one of these computers you'll need to know its address. But don't panic! You don't have to remember streams of meaningless numbers, there's an easy way. As well as this numerical IP address, each computer is given a much friendlier **domain name**. Going back to that IP address we mentioned just now, the domain name of that computer is the much more memorable **btinternet.com**. Best of all, most of the Internet programs you'll be using will store these addresses for you so that you can just recall them with a few mouse-clicks.

The function of the domain name is just to make life less complicated for Internet users. The computers themselves still use that numerical IP address. Every

Talking in dots

If you're ever in that awkward situation where you have to say a domain name out loud, use the word 'dot' to replace the dot itself, such as 'bbc dot co dot uk' for bbc.co.uk.

time you type a domain name it gets sent to another computer called a **domain name server** (DNS) which finds the 'dots and numbers' IP address using that nickname and sends it back to your computer. You won't be aware it's happening, but you'd certainly be aware if it stopped happening!

Dissecting domain names

Apart from being a lot easier to remember than numbers, domain names can also tell you whose computer you're connected to, what type of organisation they are and where the computer is located. The 'who' part is usually easy: given an address like **www.channel4.com**, the computer almost certainly belongs to the Channel 4 TV company. It's the bits that come after that (known as top-level domains) which can be interesting, see the table on the next page for a few to look out for.

American domain names stop at this point (that's one way to tell they are American). Most of the domain names in other countries have an extra dot and a country code tagged onto the end. For example,

Room for more on top

A plan has recently been announced to add a few more top-level domains to the list. So we'll soon be seeing businesses using .firm, information services using .info, consumer retailers using .store and individuals using .nom, among others.

you'll see **.uk** for United Kingdom, **.se** for Sweden, **.fr** for France, **.jp** for Japan and **.fi** for Finland.

Domain	Used by
.co	A commercial company
.com	Until recently, an American company; now also used for companies outside the States
.ac	An academic establishment (college, university, etc.)
.edu	An American college or university domain
.gov	A government agency
.mil	A military establishment
.net	An Internet access provider
.org	An organisation (as opposed to a commercial company)

Getting everything to work together

At this point you've jumped the last fence on the technical background course, and you're blazing down towards the final straight. There are just three more elements that should be mentioned – **clients, servers** and **protocols**. These are the vital ingredients that, when mixed together, give you access to all the Internet's services.

▷ The **client** is a software program that you run on your own computer to access a particular service. For example, if you want to send and receive email messages you'll need an email client. These all look and work in much the same way as any other program you use on your computer, and you can pick, choose and swap programs until you find one you like using.

▷ The **server** is a computer owned by whoever provides your Internet access, but servers work in a similar way to clients. When you're dealing with email, your email client will contact the mail server; when you want to look at a page on the World Wide Web, your Web client will ask the Web server to fetch it from wherever it is in the world and send it down the line to you.

▷ The word **protocol** popped up a couple of pages back. To mere mortals protocols are as dull as ditchwater, but they're the vital link in the chain that makes everything work. Protocols (you won't be surprised to hear) are known by bunches of initial letters like HTTP, SMTP and NNTP.

Protocol

When two computers need to communicate but don't speak the same language, they follow a set of rules called a 'protocol', just as a Czech and a Frenchman who don't speak each other's language might still be able to communicate in Spanish. For example, your email program will talk to the mail server in a language called SMTP whenever you want to send an email message.

You might need to know which protocol is which when you're setting up your Internet connection or installing new client programs, but the rest of the time it's all just technical gibberish, explained in the Glossary.

What do you need?

The first step towards getting online is to consult the check list and make sure you've got everything you need. Actually, it's a very short list: you'll need a telephone line, a computer, a modem and an Internet access account. The computer is straightforward enough: contrary to popular belief, it doesn't have to be a stunningly powerful computer, but you will get more out of the Net's multimedia aspects with a soundcard and at least 2Mb of RAM (memory) on your graphics card. There's nothing unusual about the telephone line either, but you'll need a socket fairly close to your computer so that you can plug your modem into it.

Turn off Call Waiting!

If you have the Call Waiting service on your phone line, make sure you turn it off every time you go online (by dialling # **43** #) and back on again when you've finished (* **43** #). Otherwise, an incoming call at the wrong moment could disconnect you and cancel anything you were doing (particularly irritating if you were waiting for a huge file to download and were just seconds from completion!).

The modem is the device that converts the information on a computer into sound that can be sent down a phone line, and converts it back to meaningful information again when it gets to the other end. The most important thing to look at when buying a modem is its speed – how much information it can move around per second. The faster your modem (in theory, at least), the quicker you'll get everything done that you planned to do, cutting your phone bill and any online charges as a result.

At the moment, the fastest modems shift data around at a maximum speed of 56Kbps (56 thousand bits per second). The slowest (and therefore cheapest) modem you'll find is 14.4Kbps, with a 28.8 and a 33.6 sitting in-between. A 14.4Kbps modem really is a false economy – if you connect to the Net for more than a few minutes a week at this speed you'll be miserable. It's better to go for either of the 'in-between' speeds, with models starting at under £100, but make sure you check the connection speed offered by your access provider before parting with your cash: you don't want to connect at a speed slower than that your modem can handle.

Finally on the subject of modems, you can choose between an internal or an external model. Although the external modem is slightly more expensive, it tends to be the better buy. It's much easier to install (just plug in the phone cable, serial cable, and mains plug), and the lights on the front make it easier to tell what's going on.

Is a fast modem really worth the extra money?

Generally speaking, yes it is. But you've heard the term 'superhighway' used to describe the Internet. Like any highway, there are a lot of people all trying to get to the same place and things can occasionally slow to a crawl for everyone. But, when everything's running smoothly, a 28.8Kbps modem is streets ahead of a 14.4.

With all the necessary hardware bits and bobs in place, the final thing you need is a way to connect to a computer that's a part of the Internet. There are hundreds of companies in the UK which specialise in selling dial-up links to the Internet via their own computers, so the next step is to choose one of these companies and set up an account with them.

This leads to the main decision you have to make: do you want an account with an **Internet Access Provider** (often just called an IAP) or with an **online service**?

Online services & IAPs — what's the difference?

The most important thing that access providers and the major online services have in common is that they both let you connect to the Internet. It's the way they do it and what else they have to offer that makes them different, along with their methods of deciding how much you should pay. To round off this chapter, and help you decide which path to follow, let's take a look at the two options and the pros and cons of each.

Online services

You may have heard of the 'big three' online services, **America Online** (AOL), **CompuServe** (CSi) and the **Microsoft Network** (MSN). In fact, if you buy computer magazines, you're probably snowed under with floppy disks and CD-ROMs inviting you to sign up to one or other of these. One of the main plus-points about these online services is the speed and ease with which you can sign up: just this one disk and a credit or debit card number is all you need.

But it's important not to confuse online services with the Internet itself. An online service is rather like an exclusive club: once you subscribe you'll have access to a range of members-only areas such as discussion forums, chat rooms and file libraries. Although you can 'escape' to the Internet from here, non-members can't get in. You won't find much in the members-only areas that you can't find on the Internet itself, but online services do have the combined benefits of ease of use, online help if you get lost and a friendly all-in-one program from which you can reach everything you need. Although the Internet certainly isn't the chamber of horrors that some newspapers would have you believe, there's little control over what gets published there; online services carefully filter and control their members-only content, making them the preferred choice for getting the whole family online.

Online services probably sound pretty good so far – you get the Internet, and a bit more. So what counts against them? Mainly the price. Most online services charge a low monthly subscription fee of around £6 which includes five free hours online. This is ideal for a light user, but five hours per month can pass in a flash if you plan to surf the World Wide Web or download files. Once your free hours are used up you'll be paying a premium for subsequent hours, so the online service could be an expensive option. Most services are beginning to offer alternative pricing plans though, so try to gauge how much time you're likely to spend online as you use your free first month and change to a different plan if necessary before the second month begins.

Finally, online services tend to offer Internet access as an 'extra' – when you step out onto the Net itself you might find that the information doesn't travel as quickly as it does on a direct Internet connection.

Internet Access Providers

An Internet Access Provider gives you access to the Internet, plain and simple. When you dial in to your access provider's computer, you'll see a message on the screen that tells you you're connected, but you won't feel the earth move. Instead, you'll start your email program or your Web software and begin doing whatever you wanted to do.

The IAP account has several valuable points in its favour. First, you'll only pay a single monthly charge of around £12 with no restrictions or charges for the time you spend online. Second, you'll have far greater flexibility in your choice of software. Most access providers will give you a bundle of programs when you sign up, but you don't have to use them – try some of the programs mentioned in later chapters of this book

Any suggestions?

If you can't decide whether to go for an IAP account or not, here's a suggestion: go for an online service to start with. It's easy to set up, you'll get (at least) a 30-day free trial and you can get a taste of the service itself and the Internet. If you decide later that you need the flexibility or economy of an IAP account, you can cancel whenever you like.

until you find the ones you're happy with.

IAPs have their negative side too, of course. Until quite recently, setting up your computer to connect to your IAP could be a long and frustrating business, even if you understood all the jargon. However, with growing competition among companies eager to part you from your cash, most are now sending out pre-configured software (all the complicated settings are made for you) so that you can just install it and go online straight away. Many also provide free telephone support in case you get stuck.

The effect on your phone bill

Whether you've chosen to hook up with an IAP or an online service, you'll have to dial in to that company's computer every time you want to go online. This means that if you connect for 20 minutes you'll pay for a 20-minute phone call (although it's your modem using the line, not your phone). So how much are these phone calls going to cost?

The good news is that you should always be able to connect through a local phone number. At the time of writing, British Telecom's local call rate (per minute) is 4p peak, 1.7p cheap and 1p at weekends. Add your access number to your 'Friends & Family' list and you'll save a useful 10 per cent. And if your phone bill is high enough to qualify for the Premier Line scheme you'll be able to knock off another 15 per cent. Prices change, of course, and different phone companies' charges will vary, so make sure you check these details before relying on them.

Making the Connection

In This Chapter...

▷ How to pick the best IAP for your needs

▷ The six essential questions to ask an IAP before subscribing

▷ Choosing and signing up with an online service

▷ Reaching the Internet from your online service software

Now that you've made the all-important decisions, this is where things start to happen – after following the instructions in this chapter you'll be online and ready to start exploring the Internet.

Right now you're just two steps away from connecting: you need to choose and subscribe to an access provider or online service, and install the software they give you.

Choosing an Internet Access Provider

There are countless IAPs in the UK, and more are starting up all the time. You'll find a list of some of the major UK access providers in the Directory at the back of this book. The first step is to whittle these down to a shortlist of half-a-dozen or so using the following tips as a guide:

▷ **Are they local?** You need to know the location of the computer you're dialling in to, sometimes called a 'node' or a PoP (Point of Presence) – it's the crucial factor in determining whether you should consider an IAP. You must be able to dial in using a local phone number! Many IAPs have nodes all over the UK, so you can probably include them on your list. Others might be smaller companies with, perhaps, a single computer in Blackpool. This could be ideal if you live in the Blackpool area, but if you're in Torquay, forget it.

▷ **Did someone recommend them?** If a particular IAP can offer you local access and you've heard positive things about them (in terms of reliability of connection, good telephone support, etc.), they're definitely worth adding to the shortlist.

The next step is to get on the phone. Any company that takes itself seriously will be happy to answer your questions, so pick a promising candidate from your shortlist and give them a ring. If you can't get straight answers to the following questions, either press the point harder or cross them off the list (and don't let them blind you with jargon either!).

Asking questions – six of the best

First, check any details from the list at the back of this book, and any that were given to you by another subscriber, to make sure they're accurate and up to date. Then work your way down this list:

▷ **What is your monthly subscription fee?**
A common price is about £12 including VAT. If this IAP charges more it's worth asking what else they provide that other companies don't. With many companies you can get a reduction by paying annually.

▷ **Do you charge extra for the time I spend online?**
The correct answer to this is 'No we don't'. If they get this one wrong, go no further!

▷ **What is your fastest modem connection speed?**
If you have a 28.8Kbps modem you don't want to connect at a slower speed. Many companies have upgraded to 33.6Kbps modems, and some even support the very latest 56Kbps.

▷ **Will you give me a PPP connection?** The two options are PPP or SLIP. You don't want a SLIP connection, but a few companies still use them. A PPP connection is faster, and it's easier to set up (especially in Windows 95 and later).

▷ **When is telephone support available?** You'll almost certainly need telephone support sometime, so find out whether it will be available when you're most likely to be using the Internet (for example, during evenings and weekends).

▷ **Do you provide pre-configured connection software for my computer?** Many companies will ask you questions about your computer and operating system, and then send you software that's ready to install with all the tricky stuff taken care of. (The software may be on CD-ROM, so be sure to check this if you don't have a CD-ROM drive.) Find out if the connection will be easy to set up on your computer, and whether the technical support phone line will be able to talk you through the process if you get stuck.

When you've found the access provider of your dreams, you're almost ready to subscribe. But first...

Choosing your username

When you start a subscription with an access provider, you'll be identified by your choice of **username** (some companies refer to it as a user ID, logon name or member name). You'll need to quote this when you call the support-line with a question, and when you log on to the provider's computer to surf the Internet. It also forms the unique part of your email address. If you were to start an account with **mycompany.co.uk**, you would use the following email address *username*@**mycompany.co.uk** and this is the address you'd give out to friends and colleagues so that they could send you email.

Do I have to use my own name?

No. You can use just about anything you want. It will be easier for you (and other people) to remember if it doesn't contain numbers, but there's nothing to stop you having a username like **jellyfish** or **zapdoodle**, as long as your IAP doesn't already have a zapdoodle on its subscriber list.

The rules on usernames vary a little between providers. They can't contain spaces (in common with any Internet address), but dots, dashes and underscores are usually okay. Most importantly, it must be a username that hasn't already been scooped by another subscriber to your chosen access provider, so it's worth putting a bit of thought into a second and third choice in case your first is unavailable.

And now... subscribe!

It's time to get back on the phone to your chosen provider and tell them you'd like to subscribe. The provider will set up an account for you, but exactly what happens next will depend on the individual access provider:

▷ You may receive a disk in the post that's pre-configured for your computer, operating system and account. If so, follow the instructions that accompany it and it ought to be as easy to install as any other program.

▷ You might receive a disk of software and some documentation that tells you how to install it and how to configure your computer.

Your provider should have included instructions telling you how to install the software, so this ought to be a painless step. All the same, keep that support-line number handy, just in case! You should also receive a wonderfully technical-looking list of IP addresses, domain names and so on, to accompany the software package. Even if your software is pre-configured for quick and easy installation, make sure you hang onto this list for reference – you'll need to enter some of these settings into other software you use in the future.

Choosing an online service

This should be an easy choice to make – not only is the list of online services fairly short, but most offer a free 30-day trial, so you've got nothing to lose by picking one at random. All the same, it's better to make an informed choice if you can, so let's take a slightly closer look at the three most popular online services, **CompuServe**, **America Online** and **The Microsoft Network**, and the UK-only newcomer, **Virgin Net**.

CompuServe

CompuServe has over 1,000 different areas covering just about every conceivable subject, including finance, news, TV listings, articles from popular magazines, travel information, movie and music previews along with interactive chat rooms. Many retail companies have their own forums offering advice and product support, and business users will probably find more to interest them on CompuServe than the other services. The program used to move around this lot is smart and fairly formal, although not quite as easy to get to grips with as America Online. It's also unaccountably slow in use. UK-specific content is sparse for a company with so many UK users, but CompuServe are trying to improve things in this area. Parents can download a program called Cyber Patrol to restrict kids' access to areas of CompuServe itself or the Internet, and limit the time they can spend online.

Do I have to use an online service to control my kids' access to the Internet?

Not at all. There are many good programs available that you can use with an Internet Access Provider account to restrict access to different areas of the Net, or to particular types of information. You'll learn about those programs in Chapter 10.

America Online

In comparison with CompuServe, America Online (AOL) has a very sunny, friendly and informal feel to it, thereby making it a good choice for children and inexperienced computer-users. The content provided is very similar to that of CompuServe, with a couple of differences: business content, although growing, is still far from comprehensive, but you will find plenty of UK content. Parental controls are very good, although there's currently no way to restrict how long your kids stay online. One major bonus is that AOL allows an account-holder to have up to five different member-names (AOL calls them Screen Names), which means that you can have five email addresses – good for families or small businesses. This allows everyone to receive their own personal email. More importantly perhaps for families, you can set different restrictions for different Screen Names, allowing you to bar access to areas of the service by your children without affecting your own access to the same areas.

The Microsoft Network

The Microsoft Network (or MSN) has a very stylish and modern appearance, contrasting massively with CompuServe's formality and AOL's friendliness. It also requires Windows 95 or 98, and a reasonably fast computer. MSN is 'cool', and unashamedly American in style, and this follows through to its content which is geared more towards entertainment than information. The service is primarily split into four main areas: OnStage, Essentials, Communicate and Find. The first of these splits into sub-areas called 'channels', with each channel aimed at users with particular types of interest. Parental controls do exist, but they don't match those of CompuServe or AOL – you'll have to grab Junior by the ear and drag him away. Also in contrast with those two services, MSN is an Internet-based service: when you decide to explore the rest of the Net's offerings you should find that the information travels much more speedily than both AOL and CompuServe can manage.

Virgin Net

Virgin is the new kid on the block as far as online services are concerned, and is positioning itself halfway between IAPs and the 'usual' online services. Although a range of online content is included (chiefly information and entertainment rather than business), Virgin's aim is to provide the easiest possible access to the Internet, which includes a 24-hour telephone support-line. Like MSN, Virgin Net is an Internet-based service, so you'll notice little difference in speed when you move from the members-only areas to the Net itself. Being a UK-only company, the content that is included is UK-specific, with news, sport, chat rooms and links to places of interest on the Internet.

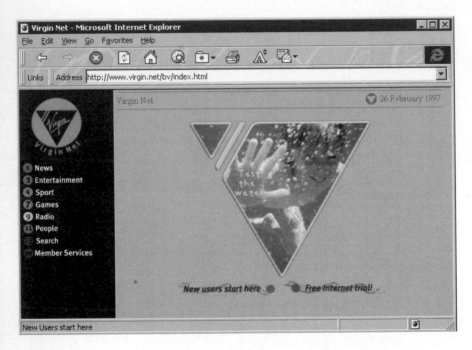

Virgin Net's simple Internet-based service

How do you sign up?

The first job is to get your hands on the free connection software. These disks are regularly glued to the covers of computer magazines so you might have dozens of them already. If you have, make sure you pick the most recent. If you haven't, either take a trip to your newsagent or phone the services and ask them to send you the correct software for your computer and operating system. You'll find their contact details in the Directory at the back of this book.

That was the tricky part! Somewhere on the disk you'll be told how to start the program that signs you up, and the whole process will advance in simple steps. The exact routine will vary from one service to another, but here are a few tips to bear in mind:

▷ Somewhere on the disk packaging you'll find a reference number (perhaps on a small label, or on the disk itself). Don't lose it – you'll have to enter this into the software to start the sign-up procedure.

▷ Make sure you've got your credit card or debit card handy. Although you won't be charged for the first 30 days' access, you'll have to enter the card number and its expiry date when you sign up.

▷ You may be asked to choose a dial-in phone number from a list covering the whole country. If so, make sure you choose a local number. (In some cases, the software will work out the best dial-in point for you, based on your own phone number, or it may use a local-rate 0845 number.)

▷ After you've entered all the necessary personal details, the program will dial up the online service's computer and set up your subscription automatically. Within a minute or two you'll receive a username and password. These are your entry-ticket, so write them down and keep them in a safe place.

Don't pass on your password

Keep your password private. Never include it in an email message, don't type it in front of anyone and make sure you change it at least once a month (you'll find instructions for this online). If possible, use a combination of letters and numbers at least five characters in length. And don't even consider using the word 'password' as your password!

How do you use an online service?

When you dial in to your online service and log on using your username and password (which should happen automatically), you won't actually be on the Internet. At the click of a few buttons you can enter chat rooms or join in with other activities and forums, and you'll find plenty of assistance if you get lost, both in help files and online support areas.

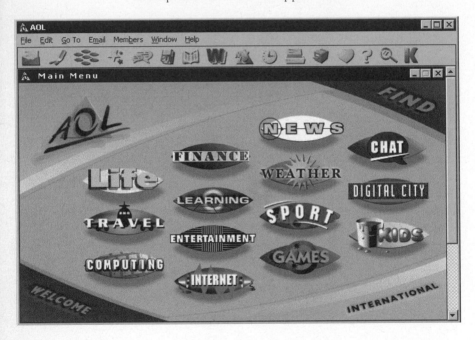

The main AOL desktop lets you click on a button to access the Internet or to use one of its own private services

Access to the Internet itself will be marked as one of the areas you can visit, and you'll probably see a big friendly button marked 'Internet' that will take you there. In most cases, any extra software needed for Internet access was installed when you signed up, but you might be told that you need to download it yourself. If so, another friendly button will probably appear in front of you and all the spadework will be done for you while you sit back and wait.

Because this is a book about the Internet we won't dwell on the members-only areas of online services.

But once you've clicked that big friendly button you're surfing the same Internet as everyone else, so the rest of the book is just as relevant to you. One of the few differences is in the way that email is handled when it's sent to and from some online service accounts, and you'll learn how to work with email in Chapter 6.

Discovering the World Wide Web

In This Chapter...

▷ Discover the amazing
   World Wide Web
▷ Learn to use your Web browser
   and start surfing
▷ Keep track of where you've
   been and where you're going
▷ Make sense of those strange
   'dot and slash' addresses

The World Wide Web is the jewel in the Internet's crown, and the whole reason for the 'Internet explosion'. A large part of the Web's popularity lies in its simplicity: you don't have to be a networking genius or a computer whiz to use it, you just point with the mouse and click.

In this chapter you'll learn the basics of finding your way around this powerful system.

Understanding the Web

The 'pages' you find on the Web contain a scattering of words that are underlined and highlighted in a different colour from the text around them. Just move your mouse-pointer onto one of these words or phrases (you'll see it change into a hand with a pointing finger as you do so) and click. Hey presto, another page opens. The entire 'web' of pages is being 'spun' by millions of people at the staggering rate of several million new pages per day, and every page includes these point-and-click links to many other pages.

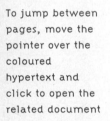

To jump between pages, move the pointer over the coloured hypertext and click to open the related document

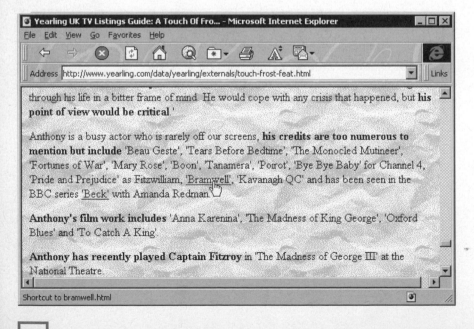

> ## 69 NET SPEAK
>
> ## Web page
>
> A 'page' is a single document that can be any length, like a document in a word-processor. Pages can contain text, graphics, sound and video-clips, together with clever effects and controls made possible by new programming languages such as Java and ActiveX.

This system of clickable text is called **hypertext**, and you've probably seen it used in Windows help-files and multimedia encyclopaedias as a neat way to make cross-references. The Web takes the system a few stages further:

▷ These links aren't restricted to opening a document stored on the same computer: you might see a page from the other side of the world.

▷ A hypertext link doesn't have to be a word or phrase: it might be a picture that you click on, or it might be a part of a larger picture, with different parts linking to different pages.

▷ The link doesn't necessarily open a new Web page: it might play a video or a sound, download an application, display a picture, run a program... the list goes on.

The Web is made up of millions of files placed on computers called Web servers, so no-one actually owns the Web itself. The Web servers are owned by many different companies, and they rent space (or give it away for free!) to anyone who wants to put their own pages on the Web. The pages are created in an easy-to-use, text-based language called **HTML** (HyperText Markup Language) which you'll learn about in Chapter 16.

Once the newly-created pages are placed on the Web server, anyone who knows their address can look at them. This partly explains why the Web became such an overnight success: a simple page can be written in minutes, so a Web site can be as up-to-date as its creator wants it to be. Many pages are updated daily, and some might even change every few minutes.

Web site

Web site is a loose term that refers to the pages belonging to an individual or company. A site might be just a single page that your Auntie Ethel wrote to share a nice fruitcake recipe, or it might be hundreds of pages belonging to a supermarket chain.

What do you need?
To view pages from the World Wide Web you'll need a program called a browser. In fact, this single program will be the most powerful weapon in your Internet arsenal, and not just because you'll be spending so much time on the Web – you can use this program to handle many of your other Internet-related tasks as well. Although there are many different browsers available, the most capable of these is Microsoft's **Internet Explorer**.

If you've recently bought a copy of Windows 95 or 98 (or a new computer with Windows already installed on it) you'll find Internet Explorer included – it may be installed on your system already, or you might have to

I'm using Netscape Navigator. Will I understand this chapter?

Netscape Navigator is another popular browser. Netscape's buttons and menus follow a very similar style and layout to those in Internet Explorer. For simplicity, we'll assume that you're using Explorer throughout this book, but you'll find the Web just as easy to navigate using Netscape.

install it yourself using the **Add/Remove Programs** applet in Windows' Control Panel.

Most IAPs can provide you with a copy of Internet Explorer, and many will do so automatically when you sign up. If you're connected through one of the online services you'll probably be able to use Internet Explorer too. Both MSN and CompuServe provide Explorer by default (although you can switch to something different if you want to). America Online and Virgin Net will let you use any browser that takes your fancy.

Start browsing

When you open Explorer, the first thing you'll see is your **Start Page**. Unlike a word-processor or a paint program, the browser must always display a document, and until you tell it which document you want to look at it will display the document set as its Start Page. By default, Explorer is set to display the first page of Microsoft's Web site.

For now this will just be a matter of idle curiosity – you've just arrived online, and you're keen and eager to explore, so we'll forget about it for a while. But it could start to get irritating later on; every time you start Explorer you'll have to wait for this page to download before you can go anywhere else! In the Customising your Browser section of Chapter 4, you'll find out how to swap this page for an entirely different one or how to replace it with another document on your own disk.

Start going home

Although Explorer calls this page the Start Page, there's a button on the toolbar with the word 'Home' beneath it. Whenever you're wandering through the Web and you get lost or you want to stop sampling the delights it has to offer, just click the Home button to return to your Start Page anytime you want to.

Anatomy of a Web page

Now it's time to get acquainted with the basic
workings of the browser and with the Web itself. If you
look at the Start Page you should see several hypertext
links (underlined, coloured text). Move your mouse-
pointer onto any link that looks interesting and click.
When you do that, your browser sends a message to
the server storing the page you want. If everything
goes according to plan, the server will respond by
sending back the requested page so that your browser
can display it.

Spend a little time following links to see where they
lead. Don't limit yourself to clicking textual links alone,
though – many of the pictures and graphics you see on
a page will lead somewhere too. Take a look at the
page shown in the following screenshot from *Time Out*
magazine's site (**http://www.timeout.co.uk**) for a few
clues to the type of thing you're likely to find on a
Web page.

Some of the main
elements that
make up a Web
page

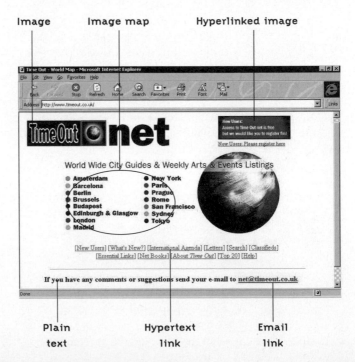

▷ **Plain text.** Ordinary, readable text. Click it all you like – nothing will happen!

▷ **Hypertext link.** A text link to another page. Hypertext links will almost always be underlined, but their text colour will vary from site to site.

▷ **Image.** A picture or graphic that enhances a Web site. Like most pictures, it paints a thousand words, but it won't lead anywhere if you click it.

▷ **Hyperlinked image.** Clicking this image will open a new page. In most cases a hyperlinked image will look no different to an ordinary image, but it may have a box around it that's the same colour as any hypertext links on the page.

▷ **Image map.** An image split up into small chunks, with each chunk leading to a different page. In this case, every city name is linked to its own page listing forthcoming events in that city.

▷ **Email link.** Click on this link and your email program will open so that you can send a message to the Web page's author. The author's address will be automatically inserted into the message for you.

The tricky thing can be to tell an ordinary image from an image that links somewhere. The solution is always to watch your mouse-pointer: when you move the pointer onto any link (image or text), it will turn into a hand shape with a pointing finger. In a well-constructed image map, the different areas of the picture itself should make it clear where each link will lead.

Charting your course on the Web

By now, you should be cheerfully clicking links of all descriptions and skipping from page to page with casual abandon. The problem is, you can only move forwards. If you find yourself heading down a blind alley, how can you retrace your steps and head off in a different direction? This is where the browser itself comes to your rescue, so let's spend some time getting acquainted with its toolbars and menus.

Internet Explorer's button bar and address bar.

1 **Back.** Clicking this button will take you back to the last page you looked at. If you keep clicking you can step all the way back to the first page you viewed this session.

2 **Forward.** After using the Back button to take a second look at a previously-viewed page, the Forward button lets you return to pages you viewed later. This button will be greyed-out if you haven't used the Back button yet.

3 **Stop.** Stops the download of a page from the server. This can be useful if a page is taking a long time to appear and you're tired of waiting, or if you clicked a link accidentally and decide you want to stay where you are.

4 **Refresh.** Clicking this tells your browser to start downloading the same page again. See 'Sometimes things go wrong...' later in this chapter for reasons why you might need to Refresh.

5 **Home.** Opens your Start Page, explained earlier in this chapter.

6 **Search.** Opens a small frame in the browser window from which you can choose a Web search site and search for pages by subject or keyword. You'll learn about searching for information on the Web in Chapter 5.

7 **Favorites.** Displays the contents of your Favorites list (see below).

8 **History.** Opens a list of the sites you've visited recently, letting you revisit one with a single click (see 'Retracing your steps with History', later in this chapter).

9 **Print.** Prints the current page. You can choose your printer and page setup from the File menu.

10 **Mail.** Opens a menu from which you can run your email or newsreader software, or open a blank form to send an email message.

One useful extra tool is a facility to search the page you're viewing for a particular word or phrase. Open the **Edit** menu, choose **Find (on this page)...** (or press Ctrl + F), and type the word you're looking for.

Many happy returns – using Favorites

One of the most powerful Explorer tools is the **Favorites** system (known as Bookmarks or Hotlists in other browsers). Any time you arrive at a page you think might be useful in the future, you can add its address to your list of Favorites and return to it anytime with a single click. To add the current page to the list, click the word **Favorites** on the menu bar and click **Add to Favorites**. A small dialog will appear giving a suggested title (you can replace this with any title you like to help you recognise it in future). To place the shortcut directly on the menu, click **OK**.

You can also organise your shortcuts into sub-menus to make them easier to find. Click the **Create in...** button and **New Folder**, then type a name for the folder. Click the folder into which you want to save the new shortcut and click the **OK** button to confirm. (If it ends up in the wrong place, don't worry! Select **Organize Favorites** from the Favorites menu and you'll be able to move, rename and delete folders and shortcuts, and create new folders.)

Click the Favorites button on the toolbar to keep your favourite sites within easy reach

If you want to reopen a page from the Favorites list, either select **Favorites** from the menu bar and click the name of the site, or click the Favorites toolbar button to open the clickable list in a small frame in the left of the browser's window, as shown in the screenshot above.

Retracing your steps with History

The History list provides a handy way of finding an elusive site that you visited recently but didn't add to your Favorites list. Internet Explorer maintains this list automatically, and you can open it by clicking the **History** button on the toolbar. The sites are grouped according to the week and day you visited a site, with the pages from each site placed into folders. You can revisit a site by picking the week and day you last viewed it, clicking the folder for that site and clicking the page you want to open. You can choose how long Explorer should store details of visited pages by clicking your way to **View | Options | General**.

The address bar & URLs

Every page on the World Wide Web has its own unique
URL. URL stands for Uniform Resource Locator, but it's
just a convoluted way of saying 'address'. You'll notice
URLs at work as you move from page to page in
Explorer: every time you open a new page, its URL
appears in the address bar below the buttons. You can
also type a URL into the address bar yourself – just
click once on the address bar to highlight the address
currently shown, type the URL of the page you want to
open and press Enter.

For example, if you want to look at today's peak-
time TV listings, type: **http://www.link-it.com/tv** into
the address bar. In a similar way, if you find the URL of
a site you'd like to visit in an email message or word-
processor document, copy it to the clipboard using
Ctrl + C, click in the address bar, and paste in the URL
by pressing Ctrl + V, then press Enter.

Accuracy is everything!

URLs are case sensitive, so make sure you observe any capital
letters. Also, in contrast with the directory-paths used in Windows
computers, URLs use forward-slashes rather than backslashes.
Actually these don't matter too much – if you forget and use the
wrong type, Explorer will know what you mean.

Understanding URLs

You'll come into contact with a lot of URLs on your
travels around the Internet, so it's worth knowing what
they mean. As a specimen to examine, let's take the
URL for the Network Chart's Top 10 singles page and
break it up into its component pieces. The URL is:
http://www.netchart.co.uk/html/topten.htm.

http://   This is one of the Internet's many
                        protocols, and it stands for
                        HyperText Transfer Protocol. It's

the system used to send Web pages around the Internet, so all Web page URLs have the **http://** prefix.

www.netchart.co.uk/ This is the name of the computer on which the required file is stored (often referred to as the **host computer**). Computers that store Web pages are called **Web servers** and their names usually begin **www**.

html/ This is the directory path to the page you want to open. Just as on your own computer, the path may consist of several directories separated by forward-slashes.

topten.htm This is the name of the file you want. The **.htm** (or **.html**) extension indicates that it's a Web page, but your browser can handle any number of different file types, as you'll see in Chapters 4 and 9.

Why is it that some URLs contain no file name?

You'll find URLs that finish with a directory name (such as **http://www.link-it.com/tv**) rather than a filename. When your browser sends this type of URL to a Web server, the server will look in the directory for a default file, often called **index.htm**. If a file exists with this name it will be sent back to your browser; if not, you'll receive a rather plain-looking hypertext list of all the files in that directory. The index file will usually be a 'Welcome' page introducing a Web site and containing links to other areas of the site.

Sometimes things go wrong...

Things don't always go smoothly when you're trying to open a Web page. To begin with, the server might not be running and you'll eventually see a message telling you that the operation 'timed out' – in other words, your browser waited a minute or so for a response from the server and doesn't think anything is going to happen. If the server is running it might be busy. In this case you might get a similar result, or you might get a part of the page and then everything seems to stop dead. You may be able to get things moving by clicking the **Refresh** button on the browser's toolbar, forcing your browser to request the document again, but be prepared to give up, visit a different Web site and try this one again later.

And then there's the Mysterious Vanishing Page syndrome. Although all Web pages contain links, sometimes the pages those links refer to no longer exist and you'll see an error-message instead. The reason is simple: on the perpetually-changing landscape of the World Wide Web, pages (and even entire sites) move elsewhere, get renamed or just disappear. In fact, the average lifespan of a site is a mere 90 days! Anyone putting links to these sites in his or her own pages has no way of knowing when this happens other than by regularly clicking all the links to check them. By the same token, some of the URLs we've included in this book may be defunct by the time you get to them. The endless arrivals and departures are a fact of Web life, but also a part of its magic.

▷ *So how does anyone find what they're looking for on the Web? Turn to Chapter 5 to find out.*

What next?

There's much more to the World Wide Web than we've covered in this chapter, but you've seen enough to know what it is and how to move around it. In the next chapter you'll go a stage further, learning how to use other features of Internet Explorer to make your Web-surfing faster, easier and more efficient.

Doing more with your Web Browser

In This Chapter...

I n Chapter 3 you learnt the basic moves that let you view Web pages, find your way around and store the location of a useful page so that you can revisit it later.

But there's a lot more to the Web than we could reasonably fit into a single chapter. In fact, there's more to it than we can fit into two chapters! To give you a good head start on the Web, we'll linger here a little longer and show you some of the ways in which your browser can power-up your surfing. Later on, you'll meet some of the 'sideshows' of the Web such as multimedia and search engines, and learn how to create your own Web pages.

Customising your browser

Let's start with some browser tips to help you fine-tune your surfing:

▷ **Customise your Start Page.** If you're content to let your browser download a page every time you run it, you can choose what that page should contain, perhaps to have the latest news stories displayed automatically. Visit **http://home.microsoft.com** and follow the instructions on the page. (If you're using Netscape, you should head off to **http://www.netscape.com/custom/index.html**.)

▷ **Use a blank Start Page.** The problem with the traditional Start Page is that Explorer will try to download it every time you start up, even if you weren't planning to go online. The other option is to use a blank page from your own disk instead. Go to **View | Options | General**, click the button marked **Use Blank**, then click **OK**.

▷ **Use a different Start Page.** You can use any page on the Web as your Start Page. Click your way to **View | Options | General**, and then either type a URL into the **Address** box, or click the **Use Current** button to set the page you're currently viewing as your Start Page.

▷ **Browse faster without images.** The actual text on a Web page downloads very fast; it's the images that you're often left waiting for, and most pages have at least one image. To skip around the Web faster, you can turn off the display of images, and have them replaced by empty boxes or small 'placeholder' icons on the page. To do this in Explorer, go to **View** | **Options** | **Advanced** and remove the checkmark from **Show Pictures**. (You can also prevent sounds and videos playing automatically, but these are still encountered relatively rarely on the Web.) If you want to view an image on a particular page, click it with the right mouse-button and choose **Show Picture**.

With the automatic display of images turned off, you can right-click the placeholder and choose Show Picture to reveal the missing image

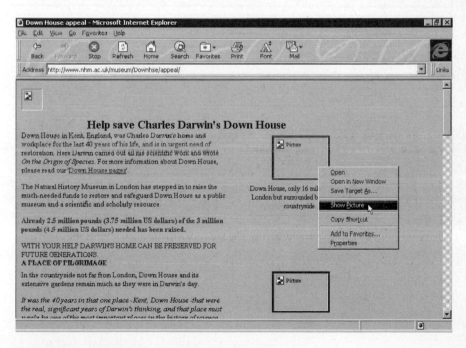

Double glazing – opening a new window

Like most recent applications, Web browsers let you open a second window (and a third, and a fourth, as long as your computer has the resources to cope) so that you can run several Web sessions at the same time. There are several reasons why you might find this useful. If you're searching for a particularly elusive piece of information, you can follow two different paths in the two windows and (perhaps) track it down a little sooner. Or you can view a page in one window while waiting for another page to finish downloading. You can close one of these windows without it affecting any of the others – as long as Internet Explorer has at least one window open, it will keep running.

Will several windows really turbo-charge my Web-surfing?

Yes and no. If you're downloading a Web page in each window, you're ultimately downloading exactly the same amount of data as you would if you used one window and opened the pages one at a time – only a faster modem will make this happen any quicker. However, if you can organise things so that one window is always downloading a page while you're reading the page in the other window, you can stop some of that waiting around.

To open a new window in Internet Explorer, you can use any of these methods:

▷ Click on **File | New | Window** or press **Ctrl + N**. The new window will start by showing the same page as your original window.

▷ Click any link with the right mouse-button and choose **Open in New Window** from the context menu.

▷ Type a URL into the address box, and then press Shift + Enter.

▷ For non-mouse-fans, press the Tab key repeatedly until the link you want to follow is highlighted, and press Shift + Enter.

Right-click for easy surfing

We've already acknowledged the existence of the right mouse-button – you can open a link in a new window or display an image represented by a placeholder by right-clicking and then selecting the appropriate option from the pop-up context-menu. The contents of the menu varies according to the type of item you've clicked, but it always contains a feast of goodies you won't find elsewhere, so don't forget to use it. Let's have a look at what some of these options do:

Clicking this	Does this
Copy Shortcut	Places the link's URL on the clipboard ready for you to paste into another application.
Add to Favorites...	Places a shortcut to this page on your Favorites menu. If you clicked the page background, the URL of the current page will be saved; if you clicked a link, the URL referred to by the link will be saved.
Set as Wallpaper	Replaces the wallpaper on your desktop with the Web page's background. This will remain on your wallpaper list as Internet Explorer Wallpaper for you to choose in future, but each wallpaper you save in this way will replace the last.
Create Shortcut	Places a shortcut to the current page on the desktop. See Using Internet Shortcuts later in this chapter to find out more about these.
Save Target As...	Downloads the file to which the link points and saves it onto your disk, but doesn't display it in the browser window. You'll be prompted to choose a location in which to save the file.
Save Picture As...	Stores the image you clicked to a directory on your hard disk. You can also drag the image off the page and onto your desktop or a hard-disk directory to save it.

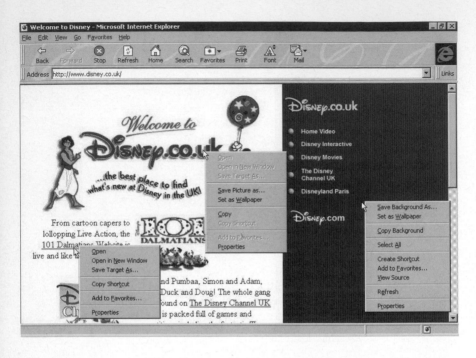

This composite screenshot shows the context menus that appear after right-clicking a link (left), an image (centre) or the page background (right) in Explorer

The last two items in the table on page 61 lead us neatly into a major area of Internet life, and a possible reason you wanted to become a part of it. There's a lot of stuff on the Web – from text-based reference material, pictures and documents to full-blown software applications – and almost all of it is available for you to download and put to your own uses. So how do you go about getting those files from the Web to your own computer?

Saving files from the Web

There are two groups of files you can grab from the World Wide Web – those that are a part of the Web page itself (such as an image), and those that aren't. The second group is huge, covering applications, sound files, videos, spreadsheets, ZIP files and a whole lot more. Although the methods of saving any file are straightforward enough, that second group is going to lead us into a few complications, so let's begin with the first.

Saving page elements

▷ **Saving the Web Page's text.** To save the text from the entire page, open the **File** menu and choose **Save File As….** Select **Plain Text** from the **Save as type** list and choose a name and location for the file. Alternatively, if you only need a portion of the text on the page, you can highlight it using the mouse, copy it to the clipboard by pressing Ctrl + C and then paste it into another application.

▷ **Saving the Web Page's source.** The source of a Web page is the text you see in your browser plus all the weird codes added by the page's author that make the page display properly. These codes belong to a language called HTML (HyperText Markup Language) which you'll learn about in Chapter 16. To save the HTML source document, follow the same routine as above, but choose **HTML** from the **Save as type** list. (If you just want to have a peep at the source, right-click the Web page's background and choose **View Source** from the context menu.)

Why would I want to save the HTML source?

As languages go, HTML is a very easy one. It might look a bit daunting on first sight, but the millions of people who have added their own pages to the Web can attest to its simplicity. Most of these people learnt the language by saving the source files of other Web-pages and then having a look at them in a text-editor. In addition, you can also open this page in your browser later to read its text offline.

▷ **Saving images from the page.** As you learnt earlier, it just takes a right-click on any image to save it to disk. You can also save the background, a small image file that the browser tiles to fill the entire viewing area. In addition to the **Set as Wallpaper** option mentioned above, you can right-click the background and choose **Save Background As...** to save the image file to the directory of your choice. You can also copy images or the background to the clipboard with a right-click, ready to paste into another application.

Saving other types of file

Although most of the links you find on Web pages will open another page, some will be links to files that you can download (don't worry – it should be obvious, and if it isn't, just hit the Cancel button as soon as you get the chance if you find yourself unexpectedly down-loading a file you don't want). As we mentioned earlier, this is where things get a bit more complicated. Come what may, the file must be downloaded to your own computer before you can do anything with it at all, but how you choose to handle the download will depend upon what you want to do with the file itself. The browser may be multi-talented, but it can't display every type of file that exists!

What it can do, however, is to launch an **external viewer** to display the file. An external viewer is just a slightly technical way of saying 'another program on your computer'. Two vital elements are required for your browser to be able to do this:

▷ You must have a program on your disk that can open or play the type of file you're about to download.

▷ The browser needs to know which program to use for a particular type of file, and where to find it on your disk.

After you click the link, Internet Explorer will start to download the file it refers to and then show the dialog below. It wants to know what to do with the file when it's finished downloading: do you want to save the file and carry on surfing, or open it immediately using an external viewer?

Internet Explorer

Opening:
ssetupex.exe from www.mste.com

Some files can contain viruses or otherwise be harmful to your computer. It is important to be certain that this file is from a trustworthy source.

What would you like to do with this file?

○ Open it
⦿ Save it to disk

☑ Always ask before opening this type of file

[OK]   [Cancel]

Explorer wants to know whether it should open this file after downloading, or save it to your hard disk

▷ **Save it to disk.** If you choose this option, Explorer will present a **Save As** dialog so that you can choose a directory to save the file into, followed by a smaller dialog that will keep you posted on the progress of the download and how much longer it should take. While the file is downloading you can wait, or continue surfing the Web, and there's a handy **Cancel** button you can use if you change your mind halfway through, or the download seems to be taking too long. The **Save it to disk** option is the best (and safest) option to use.

▷ **Open it.** For a file that you want to view or play straight away, you can click the **Open it** button. Explorer will then prompt you to choose the program you want to use, so click the **Browse** button in the next dialog to locate and double-click a program that can handle this type of file, and then click **OK**. Explorer will download the file and then launch that program to display the file. After clicking the **Open it** button, you'll see a checkbox below labelled **Always ask before opening this type of file**. If you remove the checkmark from this box, Explorer will always use the program you select whenever you download files of the same type in the future.

Virus alert!

Always run a virus-checker before running any program you've downloaded. Although people get a bit too hysterical about it, there's a small risk that a program might contain a virus. It only takes a few seconds to do and might just save a lot of hassle later. You'll find out more about viruses and virus-checkers in Chapter 9.

Configuring your browser – automatic or manual?

In the routine above, we've assumed that you do actually have a program on your own system that can play or display the type of file you're downloading. Of course, that won't always be the case. Remember that you can opt to save any file so that you know you've got it safe and sound on your disk, and then go hunting for a suitable player or viewer program afterwards. You can then install the new program in the usual way and use it to open this file.

If you do that, you have three possible options for the future:

▷ Every time you come across a file of this type on the Web you can opt to save it, and open it yourself later on in the same way.

▷ You can wait until you find another file of this type, click on **Open it** and then direct Explorer to the external viewer that you now possess. If you choose this method, your browser will configure itself automatically to use this viewer for this type of file in future.

▷ You can configure Internet Explorer yourself as soon as you've installed the new program so that it knows exactly what to do next time you choose to open this type of file.

It's easiest to go for one of the first two options. If you save the file and view it later, you won't be wasting expensive online time looking at something that will still be there when you disconnect. And if you wait until the next time you find this kind of file, you'll just have to spend a few seconds pointing Explorer to the correct viewer.

If you really do want to configure Explorer yourself, you'll need to know something about file types, extensions and the way in which particular file types are associated with a certain program. That's the sort of technical stuff we're not going to venture into here, and it's rarely necessary to configure these settings yourself when your browser makes such a good job of it.

▷ *For more on file types and viewers, skip ahead to Chapter 9. Or turn to Chapter 15 to find some of the best add-ons for viewing the Web's multimedia files.*

Using Internet Shortcuts

We've looked at a few ways that you can go to a particular page on the Web – you can click a link on a page, type a URL into the address bar and press Enter or select the site from your History list or Favorites. Another method is the **Internet Shortcut**.

An Internet Shortcut is a file containing a Web page's URL. Keep these files on your desktop (or indeed anywhere on your computer's hard disk) and double-click them to go to the page they point at. They work in exactly the same way as the links found on a Web page.

NET TIP

Internet Shortcuts are my Favorites

If you're using Internet Explorer, you'll find a directory called Favorites on your hard disk. When you open it, you'll see all the items on your Favorites menu. These are all Internet Shortcuts; you can create new shortcuts here, and add sub-directories, all of which will appear on your Favorites menu.

The easiest way to create an Internet Shortcut is to click on any link in a Web page and (before releasing the mouse-button) drag it to your desktop. You can also create your own shortcuts by hand. Open a text editor such as Windows' Notepad and type the following:

[InternetShortcut]
URL = *type the URL here*

After the equals sign, type the URL you want this shortcut to point at, such as **http://www.disney.co.uk**. Save the file wherever you like with an appropriate name and the extension **.url**. For instance, you might call this example **Disney Site.url**. To use an Internet Shortcut, just double-click it. Your browser will start and will open the page. If your browser is already running, you can drag and drop a shortcut into its window. You can also copy these shortcuts onto a floppy disk or attach them to an email message so that someone else can use them.

Finding your Way on the Web

In This Chapter...

▷ Finding Web sites using search engines and directories

▷ Tips for getting the best results from your search

▷ Locate companies and services using specialised searches

▷ Power-searching with Internet Explorer

Armed with the information we've covered in the last two chapters you're ready to venture out onto the Web and start surfing. And almost immediately you'll hit a predicament: how on earth can you find what you're looking for?

As you probably guessed, the Web is one jump ahead of you on that score. Whatever you're looking for, there's no shortage of tools to help you find it. Choosing the best tool to use will depend largely on the type of information you want, but don't panic: these search tools are easy to use, and you'll probably use several of them regularly. And all you need is your trusty browser.

Finding a search site

Anything you can find on the World Wide Web you can find a link to at one of the Web's search sites. Although finding a search site on the Web is easy, picking the one that's going to give the best results is never an exact science. Essentially, there are two types of site available: **search engines** and **directories**.

▷ Search engines are indexes of World Wide Web sites, usually built automatically by a program called a spider, a robot, a worm or something equally appetising (the AltaVista search engine uses a program it endearingly calls Scooter). These programs scour the Web constantly, and return with information about a page's location, title and contents, which is then added to an index. To search for a certain type of information, just type in keywords and the search engine will display a list of sites containing those words.

▷ Directories are hand-built lists of pages sorted into categories. Although you can search directories using a keyword search, it's often as easy to click on a category, and then click your way through the ever-more-specific sub-categories until you find the subject you're interested in.

Search engines have the benefit of being about as up-to-date in their indexes as it's possible to be, as a result of their automation. The downside is that if you search for **pancake recipe** in a search engine, the resulting list of pages won't all necessarily contain recipes for pancakes – some might just be pages in which the words 'pancake' and 'recipe' coincidentally both happen to appear. However, the robot-programs used by the search engines all vary in the ways they gather information, so you'll quite likely get results using one engine that you didn't get using another.

Directories don't have this problem because they list the subject of a page rather than the words it contains, but you won't always find the newest sites this way – sites tend to be listed in directories when their authors submit them for inclusion.

Here's a short list of popular search engines and directories to get you started. When you arrive at one of these, it's worth adding it to Internet Explorer's Favorites menu so that you can get back again whenever you need to without a lot of typing.

Search site	URL
AltaVista	http://www.altavista.digital.com
Excite	http://www.excite.com
HotBot	http://www.hotbot.com
Infoseek	http://www.infoseek.com
Lycos	http://www.lycos.com
SavvySearch	http://www.cs.colostate.edu/~ dreiling/smartform.html
WebCrawler	http://www.webcrawler.com
Yahoo! UK & Ireland	http://www.yahoo.co.uk

Using a search engine

For this example we'll use Excite, but most search engines work in exactly the same way, and look much the same too. Indeed, directories such as Yahoo and Infoseek can be used like this if you like the simplicity of keyword searches.

One for the kids

The Internet is fairly teeming with Web sites for children, and Yahoo has a sister-site called **Yahooligans** which is at **http://www.yahooligans.com**. The format is the same as Yahoo's main site, but all the links lead to pages for, or by, kids.

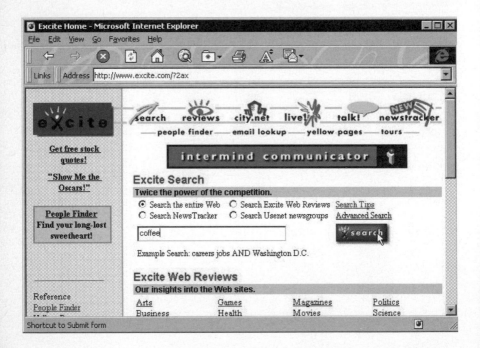

Type a keyword into the text box and click Search

When you arrive at Excite you'll see a page like the one shown in the screenshot above. For the simplest sort of search, type a single word into the text box,

and click on **Search**. If you want to search for
something that can't be encapsulated in a single word
it's worth reading the instructions – you'll probably see
a link on the page marked Help or Search Tips or
something similar – but there are a few tricks you can
use that most search engines will understand (and
those that don't will generally just ignore them).

▷ If you enter several keywords, type them in
   descending order of importance. For example, if
   you wanted to find pictures of dolphins, type
   dolphin pictures. The list will then present good
   links to dolphin sites before the rather more general
   links to sites just containing pictures.

▷ Use capital letters only if you expect to find capital
   letters. Searching for **PARIS** may find very little, but
   searching for **Paris** should find a lot. If you don't
   mind whether the word is found capitalised or not,
   use lower case only (**paris**).

▷ To find a particular phrase, enclose it in "quote
   marks". For example, a search for **"hot dog"** would
   find only pages containing this phrase and ignore
   pages that just contained one word or the other.

▷ Prefix a word with a + sign if it must be included,
   and with a – sign if it must be excluded. For
   example, to find out more about tourism in Paris,
   you might search for **paris +tourism**.

After entering the text you want to search for and
clicking the Search button, your browser will send the
information off to the engine, and within a few seconds
you should see a new page like the one pictured over
listing the sites that matched your search criteria. Using
the keyword **coffee** in this example, Excite has found
272,017 different pages. It's worth remembering that
when some search engines say they've found pages
about coffee, they've really found pages that contain
the word 'coffee' somewhere within the page's text.

Clickable search
results with
relevancy scores

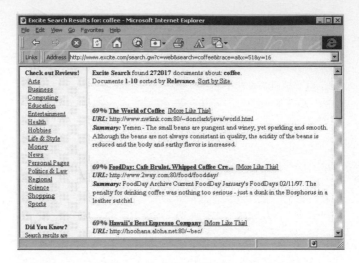

Of course, you won't find all 272,017 pages listed
here. Instead you'll see links to the ten most relevant
pages, with a few words quoted from the beginning of
each. At the bottom of the page you'll find a button
that will lead you to the next ten on the list, and so on.
In true Web style, these are all hypertext links – click
the link to open any page that sounds promising. If the
page fails to live up to that promise, use your browser's
Back button to return to the search results and try a
different one.

Most search engines give the pages a score for
relevancy, and these are worth keeping an eye on. In
many cases, a page scoring below about 70 per cent is
unlikely to give much information. If you can't find

Save your search for later

When the search results appear, you can add this page to Internet
Explorer's **Favorites** menu. Not only is the URL of the search site
stored, but also the keywords you entered for the search. It's a
handy option to remember if you don't have time to visit all the
pages found in the search straight away.

what you want using one search engine, always try
another – because their methods are different, their
results can vary dramatically.

Searching the Web directories

Top of the league of Web directories is Yahoo, which
now has a 'UK & Ireland' site at **http://www.yahoo.co.uk**.
When you first arrive at the Yahoo site, you'll see a
search-engine style text-box into which you can type
keywords if you prefer to search that way. However,
you'll also see a collection of hypertext links below
that, and these are the key to the directory system.
Starting from a choice of broad categories on this
page, you can dig more deeply into the system to find
links to more specific information.

To take an example, click on the **Computers and
Internet** link. On the next page, you'll see the list of
sub-categories, which includes **Graphics**, **Hardware**,
Multimedia, **Training**, and many more Computer- or
Internet-related subjects. Click on the Multimedia link,
and you'll see another list of multimedia-related
categories, shown in the following screenshot. Below
this list of categories, you'll see another list: these are
links to multimedia-related sites rather than more
Yahoo categories. To find out more about multimedia

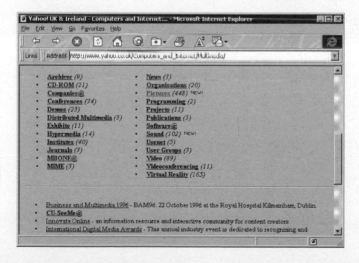

Choose a more
specific Yahoo
category from
the upper list, or
a direct link to a
Web site from
the lower

generally, you might click one of these to visit that site; to find out more about a specific area of multimedia such as sound, video or virtual reality, you'd click that category in the upper list.

The layout is easy to follow when you've browsed around for a few minutes, but Yahoo has simplified it by using bold and plain text to help you identify where you're going. Bold text means that this is a link to another Yahoo category; plain text indicates that it's a link to a page elsewhere on the Web that contains the sort of information you've been searching for. Beside most of the bold category-links, you'll also see a number in brackets, such as Pictures (448). This number tells you how many links you'll find in that category.

Why do some of the categories finish with an '@' sign?

The '@' sign indicates a cross-reference to a different main category. For example, click on Companies@ and you'll be moving from the Computers and Internet heading to the Business and Economy heading. You'll find links to multimedia companies here, but other categories will be more related to business matters than to computing.

Yellow Pages — searching for businesses

So far we've been looking at fairly general searches – you want a particular type of information and you don't mind where it is or who put it there, and consequently the results can be hit-and-miss. Searching for a specific business or service is different; either you find it or you don't. But businesses want to be found, to the extent that they'll pay to be listed in specialised 'yellow pages' directories, so these searches will almost always yield results. Two of the most useful for finding UK businesses are Yell (the Yellow Pages we all know and love, in its online incarnation), and Freepages.

Yell, at **http://www.yell.co.uk**, is an ideal place to begin a search for a UK company. Click one of the icons on the left to look for a company's Web site by category or in an alphabetical list. There's also a search engine dedicated to finding UK Web sites of all types. The EYP link on the right takes you to an automated search of the Electronic Yellow Pages: enter a company's location, and either a Business Type or Company Name, to start the search. The results mirror those you'd expect to find in the paper version. As an unusual bonus, click the centre icon to find out what films are showing at almost any cinema in the country.

The **Freepages** site, which is located at **http://www.freepages.co.uk**, is dedicated to finding companies' addresses and phone numbers, and works

The Yellow Pages online details UK companies and your pick of the flicks

Guesswork is good

If you can't trace the URL of a company's Web site, try typing a few guesses into your browser's address bar. Most companies use their own name as their domain name, so if you're looking for a company called Dodgy Goods plc, try **www.dodgygoods.com** or **www.dodgygoods.co.uk**. If you look at the company URLs given in the next few chapters, you'll see how likely this is to get a result.

in a slightly different way to Yell. Begin by entering a town or city in which the company is based. On the next page, confirm that the county listed is correct. Finally, on the third page, choose a category of business to search for from the drop-down list box. The search will return a list of all the businesses of that type in your chosen area. This is a great way to search if, for example, you need a plumber and you're currently too damp to care which plumber it is.

If you haven't found the company yet, it's either American or it doesn't want to be found! To search for US companies, you can head off to Excite at **http://www.excite.com** and click the **Yellow Pages** button. Enter a company name and category description, together with location details if known, and click the search button. If the category you chose doesn't match an Excite category, you'll be given a list of similar categories to choose from. You can also try **http://www.companiesonline.com**, a new addition to the Lycos search engine family. If you're looking for financial or performance-related information about a company, visit Infoseek and select **Company Profiles** from the drop-down list to search through almost 50,000 US companies. Finally, of course, there's the good old workhorse, Yahoo. Visit **http://www.yahoo.co.uk/ Business_and_Economy/Companies** and you'll be presented with a list of over 100 categories. The sites you'll find in Yahoo's categories cover the UK and Ireland as well as America and elsewhere.

Easy Web searching with Internet Explorer

To reach a search site quickly in the latest version of Internet Explorer, click the **Search** button on the toolbar (a globe icon with a magnifying glass). A frame will appear at the left of Explorer's window to display a mini-version of a search engine. (If you prefer to use a different engine from the one selected, you can choose it from the **Select provider** list.) Just type in your search query and click the obvious button and the results will appear in the same frame with the usual **Next 10** button at the bottom.

The benefit of this method is that you can click any entry in this list to open it in the main window without losing track of the search results. For a brief description of each site, hold your mouse-pointer over it for a moment, as shown in the screenshot above (or, in the case of Excite, click the tiny button beside a link to show or hide a description).

Explorer can keep your search results visible as you work your way through the most promising links

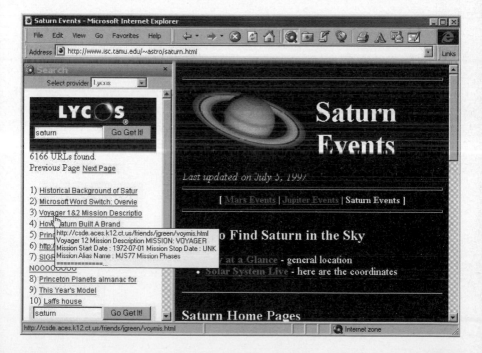

Email – Your Personal Post Office

In This Chapter...

E mail is the old man of the Internet and one of the reasons the network was constructed in the first place. It's one of the easiest areas of Net life to use, and one of the most used – for many people, sending and receiving email is their only reason for going online.

By the end of this chapter you'll be able to send email messages and computer files to millions of people all over the world (well, perhaps not all of them!) quicker than you can manage to stick a stamp on an envelope.

Why should you use email?

First, it's incredibly cheap. A single first-class stamp costs 26p and will get a letter to a single, local (in global terms) address. But for a local phone call costing 5p you can deliver dozens of email messages to all corners of the world. Second, it's amazingly fast. In some cases, your email might be received within seconds of your sending it. (It isn't always quite as fast as that, however: on occasions, when the network conspires against you, it might take several hours.) Third, it's easy to keep copies of the email you send and receive, and to sort and locate individual messages quickly.

Snail mail

A popular term for ordinary mail sent through the land-based postal service, whose speed is closer to that of a certain mollusc than email.

There's a possible fourth reason, but it should be regarded with some caution. If you agonise for hours over ordinary letter-writing, email should make life easier for you. An inherent feature of email is its informality: spelling, grammar and punctuation are tossed to the wind in favour of speed and brevity.

Everybody's first question...

Whenever the subject of email comes up with Internet beginners, the same question is guaranteed to arise within the first minute. So that you can concentrate on the rest of the chapter, let's put your mind at ease by answering it. The question is: 'What happens if email arrives for me and I'm not online to receive it?'

The answer: email arrives at your access provider's computer (their **mail server**) and waits for you to collect it. In fact, it will wait there a long time if it has to: most mail servers will delete messages that remain uncollected for several months, but if you take a week's holiday you can collect the week's email when you return.

Newbie

You're a newbie! Now, don't take offence. It just means that you're new to the Internet. You wouldn't be proud to describe yourself as a newbie, but you might want to do so when appealing for help in a newsgroup, for example, to keep responses as simple as possible.

Understanding email addresses

There are two easy ways to spot an Internet 'newbie'. The first is that their messages begin 'Dear...' and end 'Yours sincerely'. The second is that they tell you their 'email number'. Don't fall into either trap! Email is far less formal than letter-writing, and you definitely have an email address!

Email addresses consist of three elements: a username, an '@' sign and a domain name. Your username will usually be the name in which your account was set up, and the name that you log on with when you connect. The domain name is the address of your IAP or online service. For example, if your username is **bill.jones**, and your access provider's address is **virgin.net**, your email address will be **bill.jones@virgin.net**.

Quoting your email address

NET TIP

If you have to say your email address out loud, replace the dots with the word 'dot' and the @ sign with the word 'at'.

Email addresses & online services

The email address of someone using an online service is structured in a similar way, although CompuServe calls the username a 'User ID' and AOL calls it a 'Screen Name'. If you have an account with an IAP and you want to send email to an AOL member, for example, use the address *ScreenName*@aol.com. To send to a member of MSN, use *username*@msn.com.

Members of online services can also send email out onto the Internet to someone with an IAP account. In fact, for members of AOL and MSN they can use the email address without making any changes to it. If you're a CompuServe member, though, you'll have to insert the word 'Internet:' (including the colon) before the address, so an address would look something like: **internet:** *someone*@*somewhere.com*. The word 'internet' isn't case-sensitive, and it doesn't matter if you leave a space after the colon.

If you're a member of an online service, and you want to email another member of the same service, all you need to enter is the username (or User ID or Screen Name) of the person you want to email.

What do you need?

If you have an account with an online service such as CompuServe or AOL, you don't need anything more – the software you use to connect to and navigate the service has a built-in email capability. If you have an IAP account, you'll need an email client (geek-speak for 'a program that works with email'). There are many of these to choose from and your IAP might have provided one when you signed up. There are three major factors to consider when choosing an email program:

▷ It's compatible with the protocols used by your email account (we'll explain that in a moment).

▷ It will let you work offline.

▷ It will let you organise incoming and outgoing messages into separate 'folders'.

 Offline
NET SPEAK

Software that lets you work offline allows you to read and write your messages without being connected to your IAP or online service and clocking up charges. You only need to go online to send your messages and receive any new email waiting for you. The earliest email had to be written online, which is why speed mattered more than spelling.

Oh dear, more of those protocols again. This isn't too tough though. There are two protocols used to move email around: **SMTP** (Simple Mail Transport Protocol) and **POP3** (Post Office Protocol, which is currently at its third version). SMTP is the protocol used to send email messages to the server, and POP3 is (usually) the protocol used by the server to deliver messages to you. What you need to know is whether you have a POP3 email account, and your IAP should have made that quite clear. There are several dull, technical reasons why a POP3 account is better than an SMTP-only account, but the reason you care about right now is that you'll have a far wider range of email software available to choose from.

If you do have a POP3 account, the most popular email clients on the Internet are:

▷ **Outlook Express.** This is an attractive package that works hand in hand with the Internet Explorer browser, giving you a combined email and newsgroup program. In fact, when Internet

Explorer was installed on your system, this should have been installed along with it. You can check for newer versions at **http://www.microsoft.com/ie/**.

▷ **Pegasus Mail.** An excellent free program that you can download from **http://www.let.rug.nl/pegasus/ftp.html**.

▷ **Eudora Light.** This is 'postcard-ware' (it's basically free, but the author would like a picture-postcard of your home town as payment). You can download it from **http://www.eudora.com**.

If you don't have a POP3 account…

▷ **Tetrix Reader Plug.** This is simple and neat, and doubles as a newsreader program. You just type the following URL into your browser's address bar and press Enter to start the download: **ftp://sunsite.cnlabswitch.ch/mirror/winsite/win3/ winsock/trp110.zip**.

Setting up your email program

Before you can start to send and receive email, your software needs to know a bit about you and your email account. This simply involves filling in the

Entering personal email account details into Eudora Light

blanks on a setup page using some of the information given to you by your access provider. The first time you start the program it should prompt you to enter this information, but it's worth knowing where to find it in case you ever need to change it in the future.

▷ In Eudora, go to **Tools | Options**. Click the icons in the left pane to open the various option pages. The settings you're concerned with at this point are scattered over the first five pages. On the **Sending Mail** page, remove the checkmark from the **Immediate Send** box.

▷ In Pegasus, click **Tools | Options.** Click on **General Settings** and **Network Configuration** in turn.

▷ In Outlook Express, choose **Tools | Accounts** and click the **Mail** tab. To prevent the program regularly dialling up and checking for new mail, go to **Tools | Options | General** and remove the checkmark beside **Check for new messages.**

In the first two programs especially, you'll find a bewildering array of checkboxes and options. Ignore them! Just fill in the details about your email account that your IAP gave you. The rest are set at sensible defaults, leave them this way until you're sure you want to change something.

Sending an email message

You probably feel an overwhelming temptation to email everyone you know and tell them you've 'joined the club', but hold that thought for a moment. Start by sending a message to yourself instead – that way you can check that everything's working, and learn what to do when you receive a message as well.

Fire up your email program or your online service's software and click the button that opens a message window. In Eudora and Pegasus, the button shows a pen and paper; in Outlook Express the button is marked **Compose Message**.

Eudora Light's
mail message
window

Although all of these email programs look a little different, the important features are the same:

Field	Used for this information
To:	Type the email address of the person to whom you want to send the message.
CC:	Carbon Copy. If you want to send the message to several people, type one address in the **To** field and the rest in the **CC** field separated by a semi-colon and a space. All recipients will know who else received a copy of the message.
BCC:	Blind Carbon Copy. If you want to send the same message to several people and you don't want any of them to know who else is getting a copy, place their addresses in this field instead of the CC field.
From:	You'll rarely see this in the message window, and the email software will enter your email address automatically from the information you entered when you set up the program. This tells the recipient who to reply to.
Subject:	Enter a short description of your message. In some email programs you can send a message with a blank subject line, but avoid doing this. Although most people will open any email they receive (even if the subject is blank), this entry really comes into its own when the recipient is looking for this message again in six months time.

Field	Used for this information
Attached:	Lists the names of any computer files you want to send to the recipient along with the message. You'll learn about attaching files later in this chapter, see Getting attached – sending files via email..

Below these fields is the area in which you type the message itself. Because you're going to send this message to yourself, type your own email address into the To field, and anything you like in the **Subject** field (just to get into the habit!), and then write yourself a welcoming message.

Now you need to send the message. Once again, the programs differ here, but look for a button marked **Send**. Some programs will send email immediately, and try to log on to your service to do so; others add mail to a 'queue' of messages to be sent all together when you're ready to do so. You may even have two Send buttons with a choice of Send Now or Send Later.

 NET TIP

Don't hold your breath!

If your program sends and receives mail in a single operation, the email you're posting to yourself may come back to you instantly. On the other hand, it may not. Email messages usually take a few minutes to get to where they're going, and can take hours. (Days, even, in the very worst cases.)

Pegasus and Outlook Express score highly for ease of use in this department: messages you write are automatically queued, and you can click a single button that will send all mail in the queue and retrieve any incoming mail in a single operation. If you have to make a choice on an Options page about how the program should send mail, always choose to queue/send later.

If you're not sure how your program handles all this, just take a deep breath and click the Send button. (You'll have to go online first, but your email program may start your connection automatically when you click Send.) If the message really is being sent, something on the screen should tell you so. If nothing seems to be happening, look for a button or menu-option that says something like **Send Mail Now** or **Send Queued Mail**.

You have new mail!

You really feel you've arrived on the Internet when you receive your first message, but how do you know there are messages waiting for you? You don't, unfortunately – your email program has to go and look. With an online service account, you'll see an on-screen indication that new mail is waiting after you log on, and you can retrieve it by clicking the obvious button. With an IAP account, if you're using one of the email programs mentioned earlier, you'll have a button labelled something like **Check for new mail**, or you might have the more useful combined **Send & Receive All Mail** button.

Most email programs use an Inbox/Outbox system: email waiting to be sent is placed in the Outbox, and new mail will arrive in the Inbox. When new mail arrives, all you'll see is a single entry giving the subject line of the message and the name of the sender (although some programs give a wealth of information,

---

The dubious automation feature

Each of the programs mentioned here can be set to check for mail automatically at regular intervals (usually entered in minutes) and give an audible or visual prompt when new mail arrives. Useful as it sounds, this is a feature best suited to busy offices with a permanent connection (until the UK catches up with the many countries in which local phone calls are free).

including dates and times of sending and receiving the message, its size and the number of attached files). To read the message, double-click this entry.

At this point, you can decide what to do with the message. You can delete it if you want to, and until you do it will remain visible in the program's Inbox or main folder. You should also be able to print it onto paper. Good email programs allow you to create named folders to store and organise your messages more efficiently (you might, for example, want to create a Business and a Personal folder), and you can move or copy messages from the Inbox to any of these folders. In addition, you might be able to save a message as a separate file onto your hard disk or a floppy disk.

Replying & forwarding

One of the things you're most likely to do with an incoming message is to send a reply, and this is even easier than sending a brand new message. With the message open (or highlighted in your Inbox) click on the program's **Reply** button. A new message window will open with the sender's email address already inserted and the entire message copied. Copying the original message this way is known as quoting, and it's standard practice in email. The program should insert a greater-than sign (>) at the beginning of each line, and you can delete all or any of the original message that you don't need to include in the reply.

What's the point of quoting in replies?

It helps the recipient to remember what it is you're replying to. For example, if someone sends you a list of questions you can type the answer after each quoted question, saving the recipient the need to refer back to his previous message. Remember that the aim of quoting is not to build up a message containing your entire conversation, though – remove anything being quoted a second time (> >), and cut the rest down to the bare memory-jogging essentials.

The Reply button also inserts the word **Re:** to the beginning of the subject line, indicating to the recipient that it's a response to an earlier message. Although you can change the subject line of a reply, it's best not to – many email programs have search and sort facilities that can group messages according to subject (among other things), making it easy to track an earlier email 'conversation' you've long since forgotten about.

You can also send a copy of a received message to someone else, and you'll probably have a **Forward** button on the toolbar that does the job. Enter the recipient's email address and any extra message you want to add, then click the Send button. Just as in new messages, you can include **CC** or **BCC** addresses when replying or forwarding. Forwarded messages usually have **Fwd:** inserted at the start of the subject line.

Getting attached — sending files via email

Ordinary email messages are plain text (7-bit ASCII) files, and have a size limit of 64Kb. While 64Kb is an awful lot of text, it's a pretty small measure in terms of other types of computer file you might want to send with a message. And most other types of file are **binary** (8-bit) files, so you'd expect your email program just to shrug its shoulders and walk away. Until recently it would do just that, and many people still delight in telling you that attaching binary files to email messages is a job for the brave or the foolish.

It may be text to you...

Remember that a text file is just that – plain ASCII text. A formatted document created in a modern word-processor may look like ordinary text, but it needs to be encoded to be sent as an attachment. The acid test is: will the file look exactly the same if you open it in a text-editor such as Windows Notepad? If not, it's a binary file and must be encoded.

However, most modern email programs are much more capable: you choose the file or files you want to attach, your emailer converts them to ASCII ready to be sent and the recipient's emailer converts them back again at the other end. In most cases, it really should be as simple as that. The only blot on the landscape is that there are several methods used to do it, and both sender and recipient must be using the same method.

▷ **Uuencode.** The original (rather messy) conversion system for PCs. The file is converted into ASCII and, if necessary, broken up into chunks to get around the email size restriction. It looks like pure gobbledegook until converted back by a Uudecoder.

▷ **MIME.** A modern successor to Uuencoding, now also used on the Web for transferring files. It can identify the type of file you're sending and act appropriately, and the whole system works completely unaided at both ends.

▷ **BinHex.** A conversion system mostly used on Macintosh computers, similar to Uuencoding.

If you know that your software and that of your recipient both use the same system, attaching files is simple: look for a toolbar button with a paperclip symbol and click it (in Outlook Express and Pegasus you'll find the button in the message window itself).

Which method should I use?

In general, it's best to use MIME. If your email program can't handle MIME, replace it with one that can. If you have a choice of methods on your Options page, set MIME as the default. Only use a different system if your recipient doesn't have a MIME-compatible email program (and refuses to do the sensible thing!).

You can then browse your computer's directories to find and double-click any files you want to attach; the software will handle the rest itself.

Attachments in
Outlook Express
appear as file
icons. Right-click
the icon to open
or save the
attached file, or
drag it to your
desktop or a
directory on your
hard disk

Receiving attachments in incoming email should be simple, especially if your email program recognises both MIME'd and Uuencoded attachments. Eudora will decode attachments and put them in a directory called Attach; Outlook Express will show an attached file as an icon at the end of the message itself.

What else should you know about email?

Like most simple tools, email software has grown to offer a lot more than the basic requirements of writing, sending, receiving and reading. Once you feel comfortable using the program you've chosen, spend a little time reading the manual or Help files to see what else it offers. (Remember that you can keep sending yourself test-messages to find out if or how an option works.) Here's a selection of options and issues worth knowing about.

Address books

An address book is simply a list of names and email addresses. Instead of typing the recipient's address into a new message (risking mistakes and non-delivery), you can click the Address Book button and double-click the name of the intended recipient to have the address inserted for you. You may be able to add new addresses to the book by clicking on a message you've received and selecting an **Add to address book** option. Many programs will allow you to create multiple address books, or to group addresses into different categories, for speedy access to the one you want.

How can I find someone's email address?

Believe it or not, the only truly reliable way is to ask! But there are search facilities on the World Wide Web that can find people rather than places, and you'll learn where to find them and how to use them later in this chapter.

A similar option is the **address group** (known by different names in different software). You can send the same message to all the addresses listed in a group by simply double-clicking the group's name. This is an option worth investigating if you need to send an identical memo or newsletter to all the members of a team or club.

Signatures

An email 'signature' is a personal touch to round off an email message. You'll find a **Signature** option on one of your program's menus that provides a blank space for you to enter whatever text you choose, and this will be added automatically to the end of all the messages you write.

A signature commonly gives your name, and might also include the URL of your Web site if you have one, your job description and company if you're sending business mail, and a quotation or witticism. Try to resist getting carried way with this, though – eight lines is an absolute maximum for a signature.

Emoticons & acronyms

Emoticons, otherwise known as 'smilies', are little expressive faces made from standard keyboard characters used to convey feelings or to prevent a comment being misinterpreted in email messages, newsgroup postings and text-chat. As an example, you might put <g> (meaning 'grin') at the end of a line to say to the reader 'Don't take that too seriously, I'm just kidding'. Here's a little bundle of the more useful or amusing emoticons. (If you haven't come across emoticons before, look at them sideways.)

:-)	Happy	:-#)	Has a moustache
:-(	Sad	:-)>	Has a beard
:-))	Very happy	(-)	Needs a haircut
:-((	Very sad	(:-)	Bald
;-)	Wink	:-)X	Wears a bow-tie
>:-)	Evil grin	8-)	Wears glasses
:-D	Laughing	:^)	Has a broken nose/Nose put out of joint
:'-)	Crying	:-w	Speaks with forked tongue
:-O	Surprised	:-?	Smokes a pipe
:-&	Tongue-tied	:-Q	Smokes cigarettes
:-|	Unamused	*-)	Drunk or stoned
:-||	Angry	<:-)	Idiot
X-)	Cross-eyed	=:-)	Punk rocker

Acronyms came about as a result of Internet users having to compose their email while online and clocking up charges. Although messages are now mostly composed offline, these acronyms have become a part of accepted email style, and have been given new life by the emergence of online text-chat, which you'll learn about in Chapter 8.

In fact, most of these aren't acronyms at all, but they fall under the banner of TLAs (Three Letter

Communicate or confuse?

You can really go to town on these emoticons, and you could turn just about any phrase you like into an 'acronym'. Just because you know that IJBMS stands for 'I just burnt my sausages' doesn't mean that anyone else does! Similarly, an emoticon meant to indicate that you're an angry, cross-eyed punk rocker with a beard might just look as if you've sat on the keyboard.

Acronyms). Er, no, they don't all consist of three letters either.

AFAIK	As far as I know	KISS	Keep it simple, stupid
BCNU	Be seeing you	L8R	Later (or See you later)
BST	But seriously though	LOL	Laughs out loud
BTW	By the way	OAO	Over and out
FAQ	Frequently asked question(s)	OIC	Oh I see
FWIW	For what it's worth	OTOH	On the other hand
FYI	For your information	OTT	Over the top
GAL	Get a life	PITA	Pain in the a% ~#
IMO	In my opinion	ROFL	Rolls on the floor laughing
IMHO	In my humble opinion	RTFM	Read the f*%£?!# manual
IMNSHO	In my not-so-humble opinion	TIA	Thanks in advance
IOW	In other words	TNX	Thanks

Another common need in email and newsgroup messages is to emphasise particular words or phrases, since the usual methods (bold or italic text, or underlining) aren't available. This is done by surrounding the text with asterisks (*never*) or underscores (_never_).

Email netiquette

The term 'netiquette' is an abbreviation of 'Internet etiquette', a set of unwritten rules about behaviour on the Internet. In simple terms, they boil down to 'Don't waste Internet resources' and 'Don't be rude', but here are a few specific pointers to keep in mind:

NET TIP

Yes, it's electronic mail, but...

It's not supposed to look like a letter, so don't start with 'Dear...' and end with 'Yours sincerely'. You might send a message that starts 'Hi Jenny', or 'Hello John' if you really want some sort of salutation, or you might just start 'Jenny,'. But it's perfectly acceptable just to get straight into the message, and not regarded as rudeness. Similarly, you might sign off with 'Regards' or 'Best wishes', but there's no need to put anything at all but your name.

▷ Reply promptly. Because email is quick and easy, it's generally expected that a reply will arrive within a day or two, even if it's just to confirm receipt. Try to keep unanswered messages in your Inbox and move answered messages elsewhere so that you can see at a glance what's waiting to be dealt with.

▷ DON'T SHOUT! LEAVING THE CAPS LOCK KEY SWITCHED ON IS REGARDED AS 'SHOUTING', AND CAN PROMPT SOME ANGRY RESPONSES. IT DOESN'T LOOK AT ALL FRIENDLY, DOES IT?

▷ Don't forward someone's private email without their permission.

▷ Don't put anything in an email message that you wouldn't mind seeing on the nine o'clock news! Anyone can forward your email to a national newspaper, your boss, your parents, and so on, so there may be times when a phone call is preferable.

Finding people on the Net

Finding people on the Internet is a bit of a black art – after all, there are in excess of 40 million users, and few would bother to 'register' their details even if there were an established directory. So it's all a bit hit-and-miss, but let's look at a few possibilities.

Flick through the white pages

In the UK, the term Yellow Pages is synonymous with finding businesses. White pages is a type of directory listing people, and the Internet has a few 'white pages' directories that may turn up trumps. Some of these rely on people actually submitting their details voluntarily; others take the approach of searching the newsgroups and adding the email addresses of anyone posting an article. Searching white pages is just like using any other search engine, usually requiring you to enter the user's first and last names and to click on a Search button.

▷ **Bigfoot** at **http://bigfoot.co.uk.** Don't be fooled by the URL – the search engine itself is in America – but this is the directory most likely to find the email address of a UK Internet user.

▷ **Four11** at **http://www.four11.com.** The biggest and most popular 'people locator' in the States, which searches the Internet for email addresses and accepts individual submissions. Details found here may include a user's hobbies, postal address and phone number, but most entries are from the USA.

▷ **InfoSpace** at **http://www.infospace.com /info/people.htm**. Another American service, again unlikely to produce an email address for anyone living outside the States.

Are there any other white pages I can search?

On the Internet, there's always more of anything! Head off to **http://www.yahoo.com/Reference/White_Pages** for links to other white pages. You could also try The Directory Of Directories at **http://www.procd.com/hl/direct.htm** which might help you track someone down if you know something about their hobbies, interests, or occupation.

If you're prepared to wait a little while for a result, you might find them at MIT (Massachusetts Institute of Technology), which regularly scans Usenet archives to extract names and email addresses. Send an email message to **mail-server@rtfm.mit.edu**, with the text **send usenet-addresses/*name*** as the body of the message (remembering not to add your email signature on the end). Provided that the person you're trying to trace has posted a message to a newsgroup in the past, you should receive a reply containing the email address. (It's worth remembering that this will work only if the person has posted an article to Usenet using their own name; some users frequent the type of newsgroup in which it's common to post under an alias.)

Back to the search engines

Some of the popular search engines mentioned earlier have 'people-finder' options too. Lycos has a **People Find** button which leads to its own email search pages. Excite has buttons marked **People Finder** (for addresses and phone numbers) and **Email Lookup** (for email addresses). In Infoseek, click the arrow-button on the drop-down list box and choose **Email Addresses**, then type someone's name into the text box.

chapter

7

Newsgroup Discussions & Debates

In This Chapter...

▷ What are newsgroups all about?

▷ Choose a newsreader and download a list of available newsgroups

▷ Start reading (and writing) the news

▷ Send and receive binary files with news articles

News, as we generally think of it, is a collection of topical events, political embarrassments, latest gossip and so on. All of that, and more, can be found on the Internet, but it's not what the Net calls 'news'.

The newsgroups we're talking about here are more formally known as **Usenet discussion groups**; there are over 28,000 of them (and counting!) covering everything from accommodation to zebrafish.

Newsgroup discussions take place using email messages (known as **articles** or **postings**), but instead of addressing articles to an individual's email address they're addressed to a particular group. Anyone choosing to access this group can read the messages, post replies, start new topics of conversation or ask questions relating to the subject covered by the group.

How do newsgroups work?

Your access provider has a computer called a **news server** that holds articles from thousands of newsgroups that form the Usenet system. This collection of articles will be regularly updated (perhaps daily, or perhaps as often as every few minutes) to include the latest postings to the groups. Using a program called a **newsreader**, you can read articles in as many of these groups as you want to, and post your own articles in much the same way that you compose and send email messages. Messages you post will be added to the server's listings almost immediately, and will gradually trickle out to news servers around the world (the speed with which this happens depends upon how often all the other servers update themselves).

Although there are currently over 28,000 groups, you won't find every group available from your access provider. Storage space on any computer is a limited commodity so providers have to compromise. In addition, many providers are now taking a moral stance against groups involving pornography and software piracy (among others), and these are unlikely to be available. But if you really needed access to a group concerned with grape-growing in Argentina (and

one existed), most reasonable providers will subscribe
to it if you ask nicely.

If my IAP doesn't subscribe to it, how can I find out if it exists?

If you're looking for a group dedicated to tortoise farming and your
IAP doesn't seem to have one, use your browser to search the lists
of newsgroup names at the following Web sites, using the keyword
'tortoise'. If you find a useful group, ask your IAP to subscribe to it.

http://www.nova.edu/Inter-Links/usenet.html
http://www.magmacom.com/ ~ leisen/master_list.html

Newsgroup names

Newsgroup names look a lot like the domain names
we met in earlier chapters – words separated by dots.
Reading the names from left to right, they begin with a
top-level category name and gradually become more
specific. Let's start with a few of these top-level names:

Category name	Used for
comp	Computer-related groups such as **comp.windows.news**.
rec	Recreational/sports groups like **rec.arts.books.tolkien**.
sci	Science-related groups such as **sci.bio.paleontology**
misc	Just about anything – items for sale, education, investments, you name it...
soc	Social issues groups such as **soc.genealogy.nordic**.
talk	Discussions about controversial topics such as **talk.atheism** or **talk.politics.guns**.
uk	UK-only groups covering a wide range of subjects including politics, small ads, sport.

One of the largest collections of groups comes under a completely different top-level heading, **alt**. The alt groups are not an official part of the Usenet service, but are still available from almost all service providers. Because almost anyone can set up a group in the alt hierarchy they're sometimes regarded as anarchic or somehow 'naughty', but, in truth, their sole difference is that their creators chose to bypass all the red-tape involved in the Usenet process. Here's a taste of the breadth of coverage you'll find in the alt hierarchy:

alt.culture.kuwait   alt.education.disabled
alt.fan.david-bowie   alt.games.dominoes
alt.ketchup   alt.paranormal.crop-circles

What do you need?

You need two things: a program called a **newsreader** and a little bit of patience. We'll come to the second of those in a moment; first let's sort out the newsreader. These come in two flavours. First, there's the **online newsreader** – you don't want one of those! Reading and posting articles all takes place while you're connected and clocking up charges. Second is the **offline newsreader**, and that's definitely the type you want, but offline readers also vary.

Some offline readers automatically download all the unread articles in your chosen group so that you can read them and compose replies offline; the problem is that in a popular group you may have to wait for several hundred articles to download, many of which you won't be interested in. The second (and by far the best) type of offline reader just downloads the **headers** of the articles (the subject-line, date, author and size). You can select the articles you want to read, based on this information, and then reconnect to have them downloaded.

If you don't already have a good offline newsreader, here are some recommendations:

▷ **Outlook Express.** As mentioned in the previous chapter, this integrates neatly with Microsoft's

Internet Explorer browser, and gives you an email client too. If you don't already have this package, you can use your browser to download it from **http://www.microsoft.com/ie/download**.

▷ **Agent** or **Free Agent**. A popular newsreader available in two versions – one is free, the other you'll have to pay for (guess which is which!). Point your browser at **http://www.forteinc.com** to download either of these.

Having got your hands on one of these, the setting up is fairly simple. The program should prompt you for the information it needs the first time you run it, which will include your name, email address and the domain name of your news server (usually it will be **news.*accessprovider.co.uk***). You'll probably see other options and settings, but don't change anything yet.

Now switch on your patience circuits! Before you can go much further, your newsreader has to connect to the server and download a list of the newsgroups you can access. How long this takes will depend upon the number of groups available, the speed of your modem and whether you got a good connection. It might take 2 or 3 minutes, or it might take 15 or more.

While your newsreader downloads a list of groups, you'll have to sit tight and count to 10 – lots of times

That was the bad news. The good news is that you'll only need to download the group list once, as long as you don't decide later that you want to use a different newsreader. In future, when your newsreader connects to the server to download new articles, it will automatically fetch the names of any new groups that have been created and add them to the list.

Newsgroups and online services

To access newsgroups in AOL, use the keyword **newsgroups**; in CompuServe, use the Go word **usenet**. When you look at the list of groups your online service provides, many may be missing (such as the entire 'alt' hierarchy). In many cases you can access these, but you need to 'switch on' access to them yourself. For example, AOL has an Expert Add function for this. Check the Help files for details, or contact the service's support-line.

Subscribing to newsgroups

Before you can start reading and posting articles, you need to subscribe to the groups that interest you. ('Subscribing' is the term for letting your newsreader know which groups to download headers from – there are no subscription fees!) Although you can scroll your way through the thousands of groups in the list, it's easier to search for a word you'd expect to find in the group's name. In Outlook Express, click the **News groups** button on the toolbar and type a keyword into the box above the list; in Agent, click the toolbar button with the torch symbol and type a word into the dialog box.

To subscribe to a newsgroup in Outlook Express, click its name, and the **Subscribe** button. When you've subscribed to all the groups you want, click **OK**. In Agent right-click a newsgroup's name and click **Subscribe**.

▷ *If you need to find out whether a newsgroup exists on a particular topic, turn to 'Searching the newsgroups' later in this chapter to find out how to do it.*

Reading the news

When you've chosen the groups to which you want to subscribe, you're ready to download the headers from one of the groups. In Outlook Express, click the name you chose to describe your news server in the Outlook bar on the left, and then double-click the name of one of your subscribed newsgroups in the upper window. The program will connect to your news server and download the headers from articles in the selected group (shown in the next screenshot). By default, Outlook Express will download 300 headers at a time (as long as there are that many articles in the group!), but you can change this figure by going to the **Tools** menu, selecting **Options** and changing the figure shown near the top of the **Read** tab.

In Agent, click on **Group | Show | Subscribed Groups** (or click the large button marked **All Groups** until it says **Subscribed Groups**). You'll see the list of newsgroups you subscribed to, and you can double-click one to download its headers. Agent will present a dialog asking if you want to collect all the headers, or just a sample of 50. Some popular newsgroups have several thousand articles, so it's best to start with a

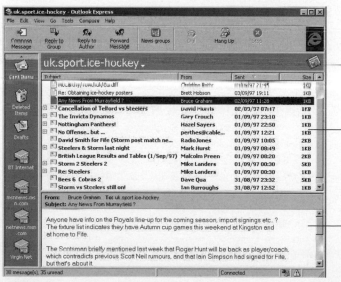

Outlook Express news

—The currently-selected newsgroup

—List of articles in the selected group

—Preview of the selected article

sample just to get a flavour of the group first. Change the figure if you want to, and then click the button marked **Sample Message Headers**.

To download and read an article immediately in the preview window, click the header once in Outlook Express, or double-click it in Agent.

Usually you'll want to download articles to read offline. Outlook Express makes this easy: just tell it which articles you want. If you want to grab every article in the group, click **Tools | Download All**. If you want selected articles, either right-click each article separately and choose **Mark Message for Download**, or hold the Ctrl key while clicking all the required articles and then right-click on any of them and choose **Mark Message for Download**. Beside the headers for messages you've marked you'll see a blue arrow indicator so that you can see what you've chosen. You can now select another group to download headers and mark those in the same way. When you've finished marking the articles you want in all groups, open the **Tools** menu and click the appropriate **Download** button.

Agent (and most other newsreaders) use similar methods. To mark a message for download in Agent, highlight it and press M, or right-click it and choose **Mark for Retrieval**. Once you've marked all the articles you want to download, click the toolbar button with the blue arrow and thunderbolt symbol and Agent will fetch them for you and mark them with a little 'page' icon.

Threads – following a conversation

Although a newsgroup is dedicated to one subject, there may be dozens (or hundreds!) of different conversations going on. Fortunately, all newsgroup articles have a subject-line just like email messages, so all messages with the same subject-line will be part of the same conversation, or, in newsgroup parlance, the same **thread**. Most newsreaders let you choose how you want to sort the list of articles (by date or by sender, for example); the best way to view them is by thread so that articles from one conversation are listed together.

Status	Subject	
⤷	[+1] **Billy Joel autog'd photo FS** (Nathan Dresler)	
	8 **Joelster** (Phu Luong)	
⤷	[+2] **Re: After the Flood** (AJ Tru Blu)	
⤷	[+1] **Wheres Billy?** (DMWMJ)	
	3 **OMA** (Walter Hubner)	
	6 **Belgium Rhythm 'n' Blues Festival** (Bob Vor Moylon)	
▽	9 **Childrens Album** (BrCr1)	
	9 CHERYL1DRJ	
	6 CrimeDawg3	
	3 **for piano-bar music lovers**............. (CIRAKLIZER)	
	218 **My Billy Joel Site!!** (Scott Crumpler)	

Click the '+' icon to reveal the rest of the thread, or the '–' icon to hide it

So how do threads work? When you post a brand new message to a newsgroup, you're starting a new thread. If someone posts a reply, their newsreader will insert the word **Re:** in the subject-line (just as in email replies). Your newsreader gathers together the original message and all replies (including replies to replies), and sorts them by date. The original message will have a little ' + ' icon beside it, indicating that it's the beginning of a thread and you can click this to reveal the other articles in the thread.

Why does this message have nothing to do with what it says in the subject-line?

Some threads go on and on for months and may eventually have nothing to do with the article that started it all, despite the subject line. All it takes is for someone to raise a slightly different point in a reply, and someone else to pick up on it in their reply, for the entire thread to veer onto a whole new course.

Marking messages
In most newsreaders, as soon as you open an article to read it, the article will be marked as **Read**. (In Outlook Express the read articles turn from bold type to normal; in Agent they turn from red to black.) You can also mark a message as Read even if you haven't read it, or mark an entire thread as Read (perhaps you read the first couple of articles and decided everyone was talking rubbish). In modern newsreaders this just acts as a useful way to remember what you've read and what

you haven't – you might just as easily delete messages you've read if you won't want to read them again.

If you want, save it!

Modern newsreaders automatically store the list of downloaded headers, and all downloaded articles, but they'll eventually delete them before they swallow up too much of your hard disk. If there are particular articles you want to keep for future reference, you can usually save them to a special folder, or to any directory on your hard disk. You should also be able to print an article, or copy it to the clipboard to be pasted into another application.

You could even mark every message in the group as Read, and tell your browser not to display messages marked this way, so that you'll only see any newer messages that appear.

Posting articles to newsgroups

It's a funny old language really. Newsgroup messages work just like email: the only difference is that the address you use is the name of a newsgroup, not an email address. But even though you send an email message, you *post* a newsgroup *article*. Don't ask why, just accept it!

Test the water first

Before posting an article to a 'proper' newsgroup where everyone can see it, you probably want to send a test-message first as you did with your email program in the previous chapter. You can send a message to **alt.test**, but it's worth checking to see if your access provider has its own 'test' group. You might even get a reply from another newcomer. Allow at least a few minutes before checking the group to see if your message is listed.

Although just reading articles can be very addictive, sooner or later you'll want to get involved. There are various ways to post articles, and they're common to just about every newsreader you'll come across. In the following list we'll take Microsoft's Outlook Express as an example, but if you're using something different you'll still have all the same options (although their precise names will vary).

▷ To reply to a message you're reading, click the **Reply to Group** button, or right-click the header and choose **Reply to Newsgroup**. (In many newsreaders, a reply is called a **Follow-up**.) A new message window will open with the name of the group already entered, and the same subject-line as the message you were reading. Type your message and click the **Post Message** button (or press **Alt + S**).

▷ To reply to the author of the article privately by email, click the **Reply to Author** button and follow the routine above. In this case the article won't be posted to the newsgroup.

▷ To reply to the newsgroup and send a copy of your reply to the author by email, go to **Compose | Reply to Newsgroup and Author**. Once again, the routine is the same as above.

▷ To create a new message (and start a new thread), click the **Compose Message** button (or press Ctrl + N) A new message window will open with the currently-selected newsgroup shown. To send to a different newsgroup, or to more than one group, click the icon beside the name to add and remove groups from the list. Enter a title for the article on the subject-line, and then write your message. Click **Post Message** to send.

In the same way as email, any replies to newsgroup articles automatically quote the original article. Make sure you delete any of the original article that doesn't need to be included. Remember that newsreaders list earlier messages in the thread in a well-organised fashion, so most people will have already read the message you're replying to.

Attachments & newsgroup articles

At the risk of being boring, let's just say this again: newsgroup articles and email messages are so similar even their mother couldn't tell them apart. A case in point is that you can send and receive computer files as part of a newsgroup article just as you can with email. So we'll assume that you've read the section on attachments in the previous chapter.

In most newsreaders, attaching a binary file to an article is a simple case of clicking a button marked **Attach File** (often marked with a paperclip icon), browsing your directories for the file you want to send and double-clicking it – your newsreader should do the rest. At the moment, the Uuencode system tends to prevail in the newsgroups, but MIME is becoming more recognised as people replace their newsreaders for newer, MIME-capable programs.

Most modern newsreaders, including those mentioned earlier in this chapter, will also decode any attachments in an article you open, with no need for

---

How can I tell if an article has an attachment by looking at the header?

Newsreaders show the number of lines in an article as part of the header information in the list. Even a long text-only article shouldn't run to more than about 60. An attached picture or sound file will usually range from about 200 up into the thousands. Only newsgroups that have the word 'binaries' somewhere in their name should have articles that include attachments, so you'll probably be expecting to find a few if you're in one of these groups. Outlook Express helpfully lists the size in kilobytes rather than the number of lines.

intervention on your part: these may be automatically saved to a directory on your computer, or you may have to click a button on the toolbar (as in Agent) to view them. Outlook Express displays news attachments as an icon at the bottom of the window in the same way as it does with those for email.

Occasionally, an attached file might be split into several messages due to its size (known as a **multi-part attachment**) and the subject lines for each message will include additions like **[1/3]**, **[2/3]** and **[3/3]** to number the parts of a 3-part file. In many newsreaders, if you try to open any one of these, it will realise that the file isn't complete and automatically download the other two as well and piece them together. In the remaining few programs, you'll have to select all three parts in advance.

Newsgroup netiquette & jargon

Newsgroups are pretty hot on netiquette, the 'rules' you should follow when using them, and Usenet has invented its own brand of weird language to go with some of these.

▷ It's good practice to lurk a while when you visit a new group (especially as a newcomer to newsgroups generally). What's 'lurking'? Reading newsgroup articles without posting any yourself. Get an idea of the tone of the group, the reactions of its participants to beginners' questions and the types of topic they cover.

▷ Before diving in and asking a question in the group, read the FAQ. This stands for Frequently Asked Question(s), and it's an article that tells you more about the group, its topics and other related groups. Many groups post their FAQ every few weeks, but if you don't see an article with 'FAQ' in its header, send a short message asking if someone could post it.

▷ Don't post 'test' articles to any newsgroup that doesn't have the word 'test' in its name.

▷ Don't post articles containing attachments to any newsgroup that doesn't have the word 'binaries' in its name. This is out of respect for people whose newsreaders give them no choice but to download every article and who don't expect to spend five minutes downloading an attachment they don't want.

▷ Don't spam! Spamming is a lovely term for sending the same article to dozens of different newsgroups, regardless of whether it's relevant. These messages are usually advertising mailshots, get-rich-quick schemes and similar stuff that no-one finds remotely interesting. The risk is greater than just being ignored though, as you might get mail-bombed – many people will take great delight in sending you thousands of email messages to teach you a lesson! So, why 'spamming'? Monty Python fans might remember a sketch about a certain brand of tinned meat... try asking for a copy of the script in **alt.fan.monty-python**!

▷ When replying to an article requesting information, or an answer to a question, it's good practice to also send the author a copy by email, in case your newsgroup reply doesn't get noticed. By the same token, if someone asks for answers by email, post your answer to the group as well – it may be of interest to others.

▷ Don't rise to flame bait! Some people delight in starting arguments, and deliberately post provocative articles. Personal attacks in newsgroups are known as 'flames', and on occasions these can get so out of hand that the whole group descends into a 'flame war', with little else going on but personal abuse.

Searching the newsgroups

There's more value to searching Usenet newsgroups than there appears at first. For example, with so many thousands of groups to choose from, a quick search for the keywords that sum up your favourite topic might help you determine the most suitable newsgroup to subscribe to. Or perhaps you need an answer to a technical question quickly – it's almost certainly been answered in a newsgroup article.

One of the best sites to use for newsgroup searches is Deja News at **http://www.dejanews.com**, which looks just like any other search engine you've come across in Chapter 5, except that there's a choice of two text boxes for keywords. If you're looking for a newsgroup, enter a keyword into the lower of the two to find groups that discuss the subject you want. If you're looking for individual articles, use the upper text box. The search results list 20 articles at a time (with the usual button at the end of the page to fetch the next 20), and include authors' details and the names of the newsgroups in which the articles were found. Click on one of the articles to read it and you'll find a handy button-bar added to the page that lets you view the topic's thread, read the next or the previous article, and post replies to the newsgroup or to the article's author by email.

Stick to what you know

If you search Deja News for newsgroups, you can click any newsgroup you find on the results list to read its articles. But, although it's possible, it's not the easiest way to navigate a newsgroup – you'll find it simpler to run your newsreader program and read the articles from the chosen group with that instead.

The great value of Deja News is that articles are available here long after they were first posted to Usenet. The only possible fly in the ointment is that the group you want may not be covered. If it isn't, head for Infoseek's search engine and choose **Usenet** from the drop-down list.

Chat & Talk — Live Conversations

In This Chapter...

I n Internet-speak, chatting and talking are two different things, but what they have in common is their immediacy: you can hold conversations with people from all over the world at a speed almost comparable with talking on the phone.

In most cases you won't know who these people are, and you may never 'meet' them again.

Reactions to this area of cyberspace vary considerably. Many people find it exciting or addictive, to the point of spending hours every day 'chatting'. Many more find it inane, frustrating or offensive. Quite simply, these services bring Internet users into the closest possible contact with each other, and are used by many to meet members of the opposite sex. However unsatisfying you might imagine cybersex to be, it's very real, and all potential 'chatters' should be aware of its existence before taking part. That being said, chatting and talking can also be sociable and fun, practical and informative – to a large extent, the choice is yours.

What are chatting & talking?

Chatting means holding live conversations with others by typing on your keyboard. You type a line or two of text into a small window and press Enter, and the text is visible almost instantly to everyone else taking part. They can then respond by typing their own messages, and you'll see their responses on your screen almost instantly. Chatting usually takes place in a chat room,

---

Doesn't everyone talk at once in a chat room?

Sometimes, yes. Sometimes no-one seems to talk at all. Sometimes there are two or three conversations going on between little groups of people, with all the messages appearing in the same window, and things can get a bit confusing. But although there may be 35 people in a room, many are just 'listening' rather than joining in.

and the room may contain just two or three people, or may contain 30 or more.

Talk is a little different. Although the method of sending messages to and fro is the same, 'talk' usually takes place between just two people, and in a more structured way. Using a talk program, you'd usually enter the email address of the person you want to talk to, and if that person is online (and willing to talk to you!) the conversation begins. To cloud the issue a bit, chat programs also allow two people to enter a private room and 'talk', and many talk programs will allow more people to join in with your conversation if you permit them to enter.

As you can see, the boundary between chat and talk is a bit smudged. Making things even more complicated is the recent arrival of **Voice on the Net** (VON), by which people can really talk to each other using microphones. Most talk programs support VON, and it's slowly being added to chat as well. Actually, this isn't all as confusing as it sounds; let's take them one at a time to see how each works.

Chat & the online services

One of the major reasons for the early popularity of online services was their built-in, easy-to-use chat systems. The major online services put a lot of effort into improving their chat facilities, and also now offer parental controls that can bar access from certain chat areas. As a measure of how seriously they regard these facilities, online services regularly enlist celebrity guest speakers to host chat sessions and answer questions. The simplicity of these chat areas makes them a good introduction to the workings of chat, even if you have an IAP account, so we'll look at the online services' offerings first.

Both AOL and CompuServe have a large button on their desktops marked **Chat** that will take you to the chat rooms, or you can use the Go or Key word 'chat'. In CompuServe this will lead to a short menu from which you can choose the General or the Adult chat forum. Click the forum of your choice and you can use the buttons on the left to switch between chat, file and message areas. The list of chat rooms shows how many people are in each room, and the Who's Here tab behind it gives a list of CompuServe members currently chatting and the rooms they're in. To enter a chat room, click its name and then choose **Participate** or **Observe** (depending upon how adventurous you're feeling!).

In AOL you'll see a menu allowing you to choose between UK and US chat. Choose either, and you'll be launched into a chat room called the New Members Lobby (although you can leave this if you choose to). You'll also see a list of chat rooms. To enter a room, double-click its name in the list. In both AOL and CompuServe you can leave a chat room by closing its window.

Chatting in AOL's Shake the Shack room

People in Room: 39

MKenny5464:	good	
TyhtyuNo5:	At least someone will talk	
SLord6free:	dont count on it!	
TyhtyuNo5:	lol	
SMitch5551:	is anybody there	
Laugher260:	hi everybody hi everybody!!!!!	
TyhtyuNo5:	Seen Jenna today?	
SLord6free:	hi Laughter!	
PookALockA:	anyone from the UK?	
Laugher260:	hello	
Ren2997917:	me	

Keep track of the conversation in this window

Type your text here and press Enter to send it

List of people in the chat room

Once inside a chat room you can watch the conversations unfold in the upper portion of the window, or participate by typing text into the space at the bottom and pressing Enter. (Don't type your username before each line – the chat program displays that automatically.) AOL shows a list of the people in the room in the top right corner; in CompuServe, click on the **Who's Here** button for a similar list. Some members fill in a Member Profile giving details such as age, location and interests which can shed some light on the people you're chatting to. In AOL double-click the name in the **People In Room** list and click the **Get Info** button; in CompuServe, click **Who's Here**, click on a name, then select **Member Profile**.

Socially challenged?

If you're of a shy disposition, you'll probably have a great time with chat. When no-one can see you (and you can easily escape if you feel foolish!) you can pretend to be anyone you like. In fact, the adoption of a whole new persona is part of the fun for many users. But if you really don't want to get involved, it can still be very entertaining just to 'lurk' and watch.

You can also invite someone to 'talk' privately. In AOL, double-click the name of the person you want to talk to in the **People In Room** list, click the **Message** button and type a short message (such as 'Do you want to talk?'). If the person accepts, a small window will open in which you can type messages back and forth. In CompuServe, click the **Private Chat** button.

Chatting on the Internet

The Internet has its own chat system called Internet Relay Chat, or **IRC**. Like all the other Internet services, you'll need to grab another piece of software to use it. One of the best, and the easiest to use, is **mIRC** from **http://www.mirc.co.uk**. The first time you run mIRC, you'll see the dialog shown in the following screenshot into which you can enter the few details needed by the program.

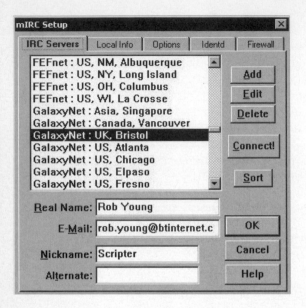

Enter your name and email address in the appropriate spaces, and choose a nickname (or **handle**) by which you'll be known in chat sessions. A nickname can be anything. It might give an indication of your hobby or job, or a clue to your (adopted?) personality, or it might just be meaningless gibberish, but it can't be more than nine characters in length. Finally choose a UK server from the list and click **OK**.

Fill in three boxes, choose a server and you're ready to start chatting

Now you're ready to connect and start chatting. Make sure you're connected to your service provider first (mIRC won't start the connection for you), and then click the thunderbolt-button at the extreme left of the toolbar. As soon as you're connected, you'll see a small dialog box listing a collection of channels that mIRC's author thought you might like to try. You could double-click one of those to enter that channel, but now is a good time to use one of the many IRC commands. Close the little list of channels, type **/list** in the box at the bottom of the main window, and then press Enter. A second window will open to display all the channels available on the server you chose (shown in the next screenshot). There could be several

Channels

In the weird world of IRC, which bases its jargon heavily on CB radio, a channel is the term for a chat room.

hundred channels, so this might take a few seconds. Beside each channel's name you'll see a figure indicating how many people are on that channel at the moment, and a brief description of the channel's current subject of discussion. Choose a channel, and double-click its list-entry to enter.

Some long-time IRC users can be a bit scathing towards newcomers, so it's best to choose a beginners' channel while you take your first faltering steps. Good channels to start with are **#beginners**, **#mirc** (for mIRC users), **#irchelp** or **#ircnewbies**. You may see some more channel names that refer to help, beginners or newbies – pick a channel that has at least six people in it already so that you won't feel too conspicuous!

When a channel window opens, you'll see your nickname listed among the channel's other occupants

The complete channel listing from GalaxyNet's Bristol server. Choose any channel from 615 possibilities!

on the right, with the conversation taking place on the left. As soon as you enter the channel, your arrival will be broadcast to everyone else (you'll see this happen when others arrive and leave), and you may receive an automated Welcome message, or someone might even say Hello. To join in with the chat, just start typing into the text box at the bottom and press Enter to send. If you want to leave a channel, type the command **/leave** and press Enter.

Q&A

How can I start chatting without 'butting in'?

Whenever you arrive in a channel there's likely to be a conversation going on. If no-one brings you into the chat, it's a good idea to 'lurk' for a few moments to see what it's all about, although it's quite acceptable to type something like 'Hi everyone, how's it going?' and you'll usually get a friendly response from someone. If you don't, follow the conversation and try to interject with something useful.

Expert chatting with IRC commands

The IRC system has a huge number of commands that you can learn and put to good use if you're really keen, and mIRC includes a general IRC help-file explaining how they work. You certainly don't need to know all of them (mIRC has toolbar buttons that replace a few), but once you feel comfortable with the system you can experiment with new ones. Here's a few of the most useful to get you started.

Type this	To do this
/help	Get general help on IRC
/list	List all the channels available on the server you're connected to
/list –min *n*	List all the channels with at least *n* people in them (replace *n* with a figure)
/join #*channel*	Enter a channel. Replace *channel* with the name of your chosen channel
/leave #*channel*	Leave the specified channel (or the channel in the current window if no channel is specified).
/quit *message*	Finish your IRC session and display a message to the channel if you enter one (see below)

Type this	To do this
/away *message*	Tell other occupants you're temporarily away from your computer, giving a message
/away	With no message, means that you're no longer away
/whois *nickname*	Get information about the specified nickname in the main window.

So what are those messages? When you quit, you might want to explain why you're leaving, by entering a command like **/quit Got to go shopping. See you later!** Similarly, if you suddenly have to leave your keyboard, you might type **/away Time for a snack. BRB** to indicate that you'll be back in a minute if anyone tries to speak to you. When you return, just type **/away** to turn off this message again.

You can also 'talk' privately to any of the participants in a channel. If you want to start a private talk with someone called Zebedee, type the command **/query Zebedee Can I talk to you in private?** (of course, the message you tag on the end is up to you). Zebedee will have the opportunity to accept or decline the talk: if he/she accepts, a separate private window will open in which the two of you can exchange messages.

Finally on the subject of chat, never give personal details other than your name, age, sex, and email address. After chatting with someone for a while, it's easy to forget that you really know nothing about them but what they've told you (and that may not be true!).

NET TIP

An easy way to make a fool of yourself

All commands start with a forward slash. If you type the command without the slash it will be displayed to all the participants in your channel, and give everyone a good giggle at your expense.

Easy window management

You can keep windows open in mIRC as long as you want to. The program places each new window on a taskbar so that you can switch between open channels and lists to your heart's content. Many people even keep several 'chats' going at once in this way!

Voice on the Net — talk really is cheap!

The sort of chat we've looked at so far is 'unplanned' – you arrive in a channel or chat room and chat to whoever happens to be there. If you get on well enough, you might invite someone else to have a private chat (or 'talk') in a separate window. But what if there's someone in particular you want to talk to? Until recently, your options were limited: you could agree to meet in a chat room at a certain time and take it from there, or you could pick up the phone.

But the latest 'big thing' on the Internet is **VON** (Voice On the Net). VON is the Internet equivalent of a telephone: you start the program, choose an email address to 'dial' and start talking. But in this case, talking is really talking. You can hold live conversations with anyone in the world by speaking into a microphone and hear their responses through your speakers or a headset.

Will they be online?

You can only talk to someone else if they're online and have their VON software running. Many American users have access to free local phone calls and can stay online all day, but if you want to contact another UK user you might still have to arrange to be online at a pre-specified time.

So how does VON differ from an ordinary telephone conversation? First and foremost, the price – because you're only dialling in to your local access provider, you're only paying for a local phone call although you may be speaking to someone in Australia. But it's the extra goodies that VON programs offer that make them valuable. Depending on the program you use, you can send computer files back and forth, hold conferences, use a whiteboard to draw sketches and diagrams and you can even take control of programs on the other party's computer. Recent programs have even made the fabled 'video phone' a reality at last – admittedly the pictures are small, rather jerky (especially with a slow modem) and a bit blurred, but you can finally see and be seen while you talk! Of course you'll need a PC-compatible video camera and software, but these can be bought for under £200.

Sounds good, what's the catch?

The downside is that the other party must also be online to receive the 'call', so you'll both pay phone charges, but even added together these could amount to less than 10 per cent of an international call charge. In fact, there are already programs such as Net2Phone (from **http://www.net2phone.com**) that allow you to dial someone's phone number rather than email address, making it possible to make cheap international calls to someone who doesn't even have an Internet account!

A second catch (at the moment) is that you must be using the same program as the person you want to talk to. If you talk to a lot of people, you might need several different programs that do the same job just because they all use different programs. Fortunately some of these programs are free, so it's probably easiest to pick a free one and then convince your friends to grab a copy themselves! Before long, the various software companies involved will probably get their act together on this as they have with the other Internet services.

What do you need?

Unlike the other services you use on the Net, VON programs have some definite hardware requirements. To begin with, you'll need a soundcard. It doesn't need to be a flashy, expensive card since the quality of these voice calls isn't high, but look out for a **full-duplex** card. You need a reasonably fast computer too (at least a 486DX, but preferably a Pentium) with a bare minimum of 8Mb RAM. And you'll need a microphone and speakers plugged into your soundcard; the quality of these doesn't matter too much and any computer peripherals store can supply them very cheaply.

NET SPEAK

Full duplex

There are two choices: full duplex and half duplex. Full duplex can record your voice while playing the incoming voice so that you can both talk at the same time (ideal for arguments, for example!). With half duplex you can either talk or listen, but not both – you'd normally switch off your microphone after speaking as an indication you'd finished (rather like saying 'Over' on a walkie-talkie).

Next there's your Internet connection and modem to consider. You might just get by with a 14.4Kbps connection, but you'll get much better results from a 28.8Kbps modem and most access providers now support this speed. Finally, of course, you need the software. There are many different programs to choose from, some of which are aimed more at business use than personal, but here's a brief selection.

▷ **PowWow.** A very friendly, free talk and VON program from Tribal Voice which we'll look at in a moment. You can download this from **http://www.tribal.com**.

▷ **PowWow For Kids.** A version of PowWow for children of up to 13, with excellent security features that filter out profanity in text-chat and warn the child when they try to contact an adult or when an adult requests a chat with them. The child will need a personal email address, however, rather than sharing yours. Visit **http://tribal.com/kids.htm** for details and download. Like the 'grown-up' version, PowWow For Kids is a free program.

▷ **NetMeeting.** Microsoft's free VON program aimed largely at business users, but (seemingly) used more by personal talkaholics. NetMeeting supports video, voice, and multi-user conferences, and you can even use programs on the other person's computer by remote control. This is installed along with Internet Explorer, or you can download it as a completely separate item from **http://www.microsoft.com/netmeeting**.

▷ **Web Phone.** A multi-talented, and very stylish, VON program based on a mobile phone design with features such as video, text-chat and answerphone, as well as four separate voice lines. After downloading, you'll need to 'activate' the evaluation copy (an unusual way of saying 'pay for') to unlock some of its smartest features, all of which can be done at **http://www.itelco.com**. Although inexpensive, Web Phone is targeted more at the business user than NetMeeting or (particularly) PowWow.

 Don't be out when the call comes in!

NET TIP

To get the most from any chat, talk or VON program, make sure you run it every time you go online; if you don't, it's like leaving your phone permanently off the hook – no-one will be able to contact you! Even if you just plan to do a bit of Web-surfing, run the program and then minimise it. If someone wants to talk, a dialog will appear to ask if you'd like to accept.

Start talking

Most VON programs have similar features, although their names and toolbar-buttons vary. It's probably an inescapable fact of life that the most popular VON programs are the free ones, so let's take a look at Tribal Voice's **PowWow** as a representative example.

When you first run PowWow you'll be prompted to enter your name, email address and a choice of password. The program will then dial up and register these in the main PowWow database and you're ready to start.

Click the **Connect** button at the left of the toolbar and type in the email address of the PowWow user you want to contact. To save their details to the Address Book for future use, fill in their name or nickname and click **Add**. Make sure you're connected to your IAP and click the **Connect** button. If the other person is online and running PowWow (and willing to speak to you, of course!), the main window will split into two and you'll see their reply. Just as in any Chat program, you simply type your side of the conversation and press Enter.

How can I tell who's online and available for chat?

It depends on the program. In some programs you can't – you have to send a request and see if you get a response. In other programs, such as NetMeeting, as soon as you connect you'll see a list of users currently online; take your courage in both hands and double-click one!

To speak to someone using your microphone, click the Voice button. Although PowWow lets you text-chat with up to seven people, you'll only be able to have a voice conversation with one at a time. Here's a brief rundown of features you'll find in PowWow (and most other VON programs):

▷ Transfer files by clicking the **Send File** button and choosing a file to send. You can continue to talk while the file is being transferred.

▷ Set up an Answering Machine message that will be sent to anyone trying to contact you when you're unavailable. Some programs, such as Web Phone, can also record messages left by anyone trying to contact you.

▷ Send a picture of yourself to the other user by entering its location in PowWow's setup page. Most programs can send images to be displayed on the other user's screen without interrupting the conversation.

▷ Click the **Whiteboard** button to collaborate in drawing pictures using a similar set of tools to those found in Windows Paint.

▷ Host a conference with up to 50 people taking part in text chat.

▷ If you have your own Web site, you can add a PowWow link to your page to tell visitors that you're online and available to chat. Visitors to the page can click the link to start their own software and invite you to talk.

▷ Stuck for someone to call? Click the **White Pages** button in PowWow and your Web browser will open the main Tribal Voice page. Click a button to see a list of users currently online, then click one of the names to request a chat.

▷ Punctuate your chat with WAV audio files by clicking the **Sound** button. PowWow comes with its own set of sound files such as 'Applause', 'Hi', 'Cool' and 'Bye', and lets you choose between a male or female voice. Provided the same sound file is on the other person's system too, you'll both hear it.

The Ultimate Software Store

In This Chapter...

⇨ Explore the top software collections on the Web

⇨ Organise your directories and simplify your life

⇨ Working with compressed archives and installing software

⇨ Viruses – what are the risks, and how can you avoid them?

⇨ The most popular file types on the Net, and the Top 5 file viewers

The Internet is knee-deep in software, and much of it is free. In the last few chapters you've discovered some of the best Internet programs and utilities, but these are just the tip of the software iceberg; you can find just about any type of file you want, from screensavers to word-processors and icons to personal organisers.

And with just a single click, you can download them and start using them immediately.

The Internet is reckoned to be the software supply-line of the future. Within a year or two, we'll be purchasing and downloading almost all our software over the Internet, and programs will update themselves automatically when newer versions and improvements become available. (In fact, Windows 98 provides this 'self-updating' facility already.) One bonus of this is that software should become much cheaper by removing the middleman and the need for flashy packaging. The downside, as you're sure to discover soon, is that you'll spend all the savings you make on ever-larger hard disks to hold all these goodies!

Shareware, freeware, everyware

Every piece of software you find on the Internet is something-ware, and the two terms you'll come across the most are **freeware** and **shareware**. Freeware is easily explained – it's free! If you like it, you keep it, no questions asked. There are usually a few limitations, though: the author will generally retain copyright, and you won't be allowed to sell copies to anyone.

Shareware is an economical method of selling software that bypasses packaging, advertising and distribution costs, resulting in a much cheaper product for us and a much easier life for its author. The most important benefit of the shareware concept is that you get the opportunity to try out the software before you buy it, but the understanding is that you should pay for it if you continue to use it beyond the specified trial period (known as **registering** the software). In return for registering, you'll normally receive the latest version, and you might be entitled to free upgrades as they become available. Apart from shareware and freeware, there are a few more terms you'll come across in reference to software.

Term	Meaning
Postcard-ware	Instead of paying for the software, you send the author a picture postcard of your home town.
Nagware	A type of shareware program that nags you to register it by regularly displaying a little 'Buy Me' dialog that has to be clicked to make it go away. Only money can stop it doing that.
Crippleware	The software is crippled in some way that prevents you making full use of it until you pay, usually by removing the options to save or print anything you create with it. Sometimes more formally referred to as save-disabled.
Time-limited	You have full use of the program for a set period (usually 30 days) after which the software won't run until you enter a valid registration number.
Alpha versions	These are very early versions of a program which may (or may not) be unreliable, but are released to anyone willing to try them. The author hopes that you'll report any problems you find so that they can be fixed. Unless you're a very experienced computer-user, avoid any software labelled as an alpha.
Beta versions	Later, and usually more stable, versions of a program than alphas, but still not regarded as a saleable product. You might prefer to wait a little longer for the finished article.

Most of the software you download will include several text files that you can read in a text editor such as Windows Notepad or any word-processor. Keep a lookout for a file called **Readme.txt** or **Register.txt** that will tell you about any limitations of use, provide installation details and explain where and how to register the software.

Where can you find software?

The best places to find software are all on the World Wide Web. Most of the software sites on the Web use a directory layout from which you select the type of software you're looking for, browse through a list of software titles and descriptions, and click a link to start downloading the file you want. (For more on downloading files with your browser, skip back to Chapter 4.) Here's a quickfire list of some of the best software sites on the Web:

Mirror site

The most popular Web sites are those that give something away, and software sites are top of that list. If everyone had to visit the same site, that server would slow to a crawl and no-one would be able to download anything. So exactly the same collection of files is placed on other servers around the world to spread the load, and these are called mirrors. When you get a choice of sites to download from, you'll usually get the quickest results by choosing the site geographically closest to you.

▷ **Tucows.** The definitive site when you want to find Internet applications for Windows. Tucows has mirror sites all over the world, but try visiting **http://tucows.cableinet.net** for a good, responsive connection. And a few pictures of cows.

▷ **Shareware.com.** One of the best sites for software of all types, located at **http://www.shareware.com**. This has a keyword search facility to help you track down a particular program by name, or a type of program.

▷ **Windows95.com.** An excellent site providing all kinds of software for Windows 95 and later, found at **http://www.windows95.com**.

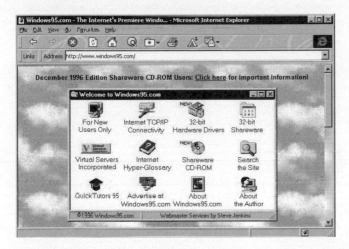

Navigate the Windows95.com site by clicking icons instead of dull hypertext links

Apart from directories of software, there are a number of other avenues worth exploring. If you visit **http://www.yahoo.com/Computers_and_Internet /Software/Shareware** you'll find a long list of links to shareware pages, most accompanied by useful descriptions. Or go to one of the search engines mentioned in Chapter 5 and use the keyword **software** or **shareware**. If there's a particular type of program you're looking for, such as an appointments calendar, try searching for **freeware shareware + calendar**.

Shareware news by email

If you want to keep up with the latest shareware releases, hop over to **http://www.shareware.com/SW/Subscribe/?swd**, type your email address into the box, and click the **Subscribe** button. Every week you'll receive an email message listing the most popular downloads at Shareware.com and details of the latest arrivals.

Downloading – choose your directory

If you plan to download a lot of software, it helps to create a few directories first to keep things organised. How you choose to do this is up to you, of course, but here's a suggestion you might like to follow. First, create a new directory on your hard disk called **Internet**. Then open that directory and create three subdirectories called **Download**, **Temp** and **Store**. You might want to choose different names for the directories, but here's how they're used:

Directory	Use
Internet	Simply a handy container for the other three directories.
Download	When you click a file to download in your browser and choose to save it to disk, the browser will ask you to choose a directory to save into. Choose this directory. When you've used this directory once, it will automatically be offered to you for future downloads.
Temp	Almost all of the programs you download will be in compressed archives.In some cases, before you can start to install the software it has to be uncompressed, and the Temp folder provides somewhere to put those uncompressed files. As soon as the software has been installed you can delete the contents of the Temp folder.
Store	You may want to keep some of the compressed files you download. Move them from Download into this directory when you've finished uncompressing and installing them so that you'll know they've been dealt with.

What are compressed archives?

If you wanted to send several small packages to someone through the post, you'd probably put them all in a box and send that for simplicity. An archive works in a similar way – it's a type of file that contains other files, making them easy to move around on the Internet.

Most of the software you download will consist of several files, including the program itself, a Help file, text files that tell you how to register and so on. Downloading a single archive that contains the whole package is far simpler than downloading a dozen separate files one at a time. Before you can use the files in the archive they have to be extracted from it, which is where your Temp directory comes into play.

Most archives are also compressed. Using clever software trickery, files can be squeezed into these archives so that they take up much less space – sometimes only a few per cent of their original size – which means that downloading an archive will be a much quicker job than downloading its constituent files individually. When you extract the files from the archive, they'll be automatically uncompressed at the same time.

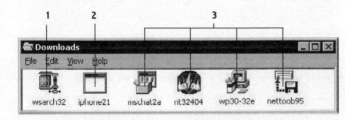

Archive files are easy to recognise by their icons

There are a few different types of archive, but all are easy to handle, and you'll be able to recognise them by their icons, which are shown in the screenshot above.

1   A ZIP archive – these files have the file extension **.zip**. You'll come across a lot of these, and they may contain just one file or many. You'll need a special program to extract the files from a ZIP archive, and the best of the lot is called WinZip (shown in the following screenshot) which you can download from **http://www.winzip.com**. It's very easy to use, and includes good Help files.

2   This is an MS-DOS self-extracting archive with the extension **.exe**. Copy this file into your Temp directory, double-click it and its contents will be automatically extracted and placed in the same directory.

3   These are all types of self-extracting archive, also with the **.exe** extension, but they're even easier than **2**. Double-click the file's icon, and everything should happen automatically. The files will be extracted, the setup program will run to install the software and the program should then delete the extracted files to clean up any mess it made.

View and extract the contents of an archive using WinZip

Name	Date	Time	Size	Ratio	Packed	Path
common.txt	28/07/95	21:14	3,858	50%	1,933	
complete.wav	14/07/95	00:00	12,106	0%	12,106	
connect.wav	19/08/95	09:33	14,354	10%	12,892	
error.wav	10/04/95	22:30	9,996	19%	8,110	
whatsnew.txt	19/08/95	17:36	6,652	60%	2,658	
ws_ftp.ext	19/08/95	13:44	80	26%	59	
ws_ftp.hlp	23/07/94	21:03	44,998	28%	32,285	
ws_ftp.ini	21/01/95	08:06	2,103	60%	838	
ws_ftp32.exe	19/08/95	17:31	230,912	50%	115,575	
ws_ftp32.txt	31/07/95	20:08	9,607	60%	3,870	

WinZip - ws_ftp32.zip — File / Actions / Options / Help — New, Open, Favorites, Add, Extract, View, CheckOut, Wizard — Selected 0 files, 0 bytes — Total 10 files, 327KB

What is a file extension?

A group of three (or sometimes more) characters at the end of a filename, preceded by a dot. For the file **readme.txt** the extension is **.txt**. The extension tells you and your computer what type of file it is, which determines what type of program is needed to open that file.

There are several other types of archive, and they'll get a mention later in the chapter, but almost every piece of software you download will either be a **.zip** or an **.exe** archive. Archive files don't just contain programs, though – you might find a collection of pictures or icons gathered together into an archive, or word-processor documents, or sound and video clips – their portability and smaller size make them the favourite way to transfer all types of file over the Internet.

Installing your new program

Before you start to install any software you've downloaded, your first job should be to check it for viruses, and we'll discuss those in a moment. What you do next depends upon the type of file you downloaded. If it's a ZIP file, use WinZip to extract its contents to your Temp directory; if it's an MS-DOS self-extracting file, copy it to your Temp directory and double-click it. Next, have a look in your Temp directory for a file called **install.exe** or **setup.exe**. If you see one of these, double-click it and follow any onscreen instructions to install the software. If you can't see one of these files, the software probably doesn't have an automatic setup program. Create a new directory somewhere, move the files into it, and create a shortcut to the program on your Start Menu or in Program Manager for easy access. With the new program installed, you can delete all those extracted files in your Temp directory.

The other types of self-extracting archive just need a double-click. Usually their setup program will run automatically and you can just follow the instructions to complete the installation.

What if you don't like the software and want to uninstall it? If the software had its own setup program that installed it for you, the same program can usually uninstall it too – look in its directory for a file called **uninstall.exe** and double-click it. If there isn't one, run the **install** or **setup** program again to see if there's a button marked Uninstall (if there isn't, click Cancel). Failing that, Windows may be able to uninstall it for you. Open **Control Panel**, double-click **Add/Remove**

Close programs first

Before you install any new software, it's a good idea to close any programs you're running (some setup programs remind you to do this). Sometimes the setup program needs to alter existing files on your computer while installing the software, and if another program is running it might not be able to do so.

Programs and see if this program is on the list; if it is, select it and click the **Add/Remove** button to uninstall it. If you simply created a new directory and copied the program files into it, you can delete the directory and its contents, and remove any shortcuts you added.

Scanning for viruses

The risk from viruses on the Internet is small, far less significant than some of the hysterical chatter would have you believe. And if you are unfortunate enough to get a virus on your computer, it won't necessarily be harmful – some viruses are jokey little things that do no more than make your computer go beep once a year. But there are others that can make a nasty mess of your system by trashing your files, swallowing your disk space, and filling your memory, and these are definitely best avoided. They're also easily avoided.

What is a virus?

A virus is a small piece of code that is maliciously inserted into an ordinary program. When the program is run, the virus starts running too, and begins to do whatever it was programmed to do. Viruses can replicate themselves and often invade other programs.

There are two popular virus-checking programs in wide use, and both can be downloaded from the

Internet. One is McAfee VirusScan, available from **http://www.mcafee.com**, and the other is Norton AntiVirus from **http://www.symantec.com /avcenter/index.html**. Which of these you choose doesn't really matter, but what does matter is that you update it every couple of months to make sure you're protected from the latest viruses.

McAfee VirusScan, a simple but effective virus checker

So, what sort of files should you scan for viruses? Any file with an .exe extension, including self-extracting archives. After extracting files from a ZIP archive, always virus check any .exe files it contained before you run them. You should also check any files that can contain little 'macro' programs, such as Microsoft Word documents. Files that are simply displayed by a program (such as a picture, video or a plain text file) are safe. Virus-checking software will tell you if a file contains a virus, and can usually 'kill' any it finds at the click of a button. If you're unsure whether a particular file constitutes a risk, virus-check it – it takes only a few seconds.

What are all those file types?

So far, we've only looked at downloading programs from the Net, but you'll find many different types of file there – documents, sounds, videos, images, and a lot more. Clicking a link to any file will download it regardless of what type of file it is, and your browser will ask you whether you want to open it immediately or save it to disk to look at later (as we discussed in Chapter 4). But first you'll need to be able to recognise these different types of file by their extension and make sure you've got a program that can display them.

The list of computer file extensions is almost endless, but here's a brief description of the file extensions you're most likely to find on the Net. Some of these can be displayed or played by your browser itself, and many are compatible with programs included with Windows.

You'll notice that some of these files have two slightly different extensions (such as **.htm** and **.html**, or **.jpg** and **.jpeg**). This is simply because MS-DOS and Windows 3.11 can't work with four-character extensions, so shorter versions are used instead. The file types are exactly the same, so don't worry if some of the files you download have a **.jpg** extension and others have **.jpeg**.

The Top 5 – complete your software arsenal!

A few of the file types listed in the table below can't be viewed or played by any program included with

File extension	Description of file type
.arc, .arj	Two older types of compressed archive, similar to ZIP files.
.avi	A Video For Windows file. ActiveMovie, included with Explorer, will play these automatically.
.bmp, .pcx	Bitmap files. View these in Windows Paint or Paintbrush.
.doc	A Microsoft Word document. If you don't have Word you can use Windows' WordPad (although you may lose some of the document's formatting) or search **www.microsoft.com** for a viewer called WordView.
.flc, .fli, .aas	Animation files.

File extension	Description of file type
.gif, .jpg, .jpeg, .jpe, .jfif	Image files often used in Web pages, and displayed by your browser.
.gz, .gzip	Another, less common, type of compressed archive.
.htm, .html	World Wide Web documents (better known as 'pages').
.mid, .rmi	MIDI files, a type of compact sound file. Internet Explorer will handle these itself, or you can use Media Player.
.mov, .qt	A QuickTime movie file.
.mpg, .mpeg, .mpe	An MPEG video.
.mp2	An MPEG audio file.
.pdf	Portable Document Format, a hypertext document similar to Web pages that can be read only by Adobe Acrobat.
.ra, .ram	A RealAudio sound file.
.rtf	A Rich Text document that can be read in almost any Windows word-processor.
.tar	Yet another type of compressed archive.
.txt, .text	A plain text file. Your browser should display these, or you can read them in Windows Notepad or any word-processor.
.wav	A Windows wave audio sound. Your browser will play these automatically, or you can use Media Player or Sound Recorder.
.wrl	A VRML (virtual reality) 3D object. We'll look at virtual reality in Chapter 15.

Windows – you'll need to find a separate program if you download files of these types. Without further ado, here are the Top 5 recommended accessories and viewers which, between them, will leave you ready for almost anything the Internet can throw at you.

▷ **WinZip** from **http://www.winzip.com**. Apart from handling ZIP files, WinZip will extract files from almost any type of compressed archive, and can also decode Uuencode or MIME attachments sometimes included in email messages and newsgroup articles. Don't even stop to think about it – you need this program as soon as you hit the Net!

▷ **LView Pro** from **http://www.lview.com**. A fast and easy image file viewer that supports all the popular file formats, as well as some of the not-so-popular ones. LView can also create contact sheets containing multiple images, or display them one at a time as a slideshow.

▷ **RealAudio Player** from **http://www.realaudio.com**. RealAudio is a streaming audio format. Many Web sites now have RealAudio sound, and some radio stations use it to transmit live over the Internet. This type of program is known as a plug-in because it automatically 'plugs itself into' your browser and waits invisibly in the background until it's needed. You'll learn more about plug-ins in Chapter 15.

Streaming

You'll come across the terms 'streaming audio' and 'streaming video'. Streaming means that the file will start to play almost as soon as you click the link to it; you can watch or listen to it while it downloads instead of having to wait until the download has finished.

▷ **Net Toob** from **http://www.nettoob.com**. A live streaming MPEG video player which you can also use to play MPEG videos that you've already downloaded or found elsewhere. MPEG is the most popular video format on the Internet, and Net Toob handles it better than anything else around. It can also play most of the other video and sound formats mentioned in the list above!

▷ **Acrobat Reader** from **http://www.adobe.com**. PDF is a popular format for text-based documents such as help files, magazines, and research literature. Documents can include embedded images and fonts, together with hyperlinks to help you navigate long documents easily.

Some of the other types of file covered in this chapter can be played in a Windows program, but you have to wait for the file to download, find and double-click it, which rather spoils the surfing experience. In Chapter 15, we'll look at some of the other multimedia plug-ins and viewers you can add to your system that add the necessary capabilities to your browser itself

Safety & Security Online

In This Chapter...

▷ Keep your kids safe on the Internet

▷ The truth about credit card security on the Net

▷ Are cookies really dangerous?

▷ Email – privacy & encryption

Safety, or the lack of it, is a much-hyped area of Internet life. According to many press articles, as soon as you go online you're going to be faced with a barrage of pornography, your credit card number will be stolen, your personal email messages will be published far and wide, and your children will be at the mercy of paedophile rings.

Of course, articles like these make good news stories. Much more interesting than 'Child surfs Internet, sees no pornography', for example. In this chapter we'll tackle the most frequently-asked questions, sort out what the risks actually are and what you can do to minimise them.

Will my kids be safe on the Net?

The Internet has its fair share of sex and smut, just as it has motoring, cookery, sports, films and so on. We won't pretend that your kids can't come into contact with explicit images and language, but there are two important points to note. First, you're no more likely to stumble upon pornography while looking for a sports site than you are to stumble upon film reviews or recipes. If you want to find that sort of content, you have to go looking for it. Second, most of the sexually explicit sites on the World Wide Web are private – to get inside you need a credit card. Nevertheless, there are dangers on the Net, and given unrestricted freedom, your kids may come into contact with unsuitable material.

What sort of material could my kids find?

On the Web, the front pages of those private sites are accessible to all, and some contain images and language designed to titillate, and to part you from some cash. The Web's search engines are another risk – enter the wrong keywords (or the right keywords, depending on your viewpoint) and you'll be presented with direct links to explicit sites accompanied by colourful descriptions.

However, these are not good reasons to deny children access to the Internet. Quite simply, the Internet is a fact of life that isn't going to go away, and will feature more strongly in our children's lives than it presently does in our own. More and more schools are recognising this, and are promoting use of the Internet in homework and class projects. The wealth of Web sites created by and for children is a great indicator of their active participation in the growth of the Net.

Rather than depriving children of this incredible resource, agree a few ground rules at the outset: when they can surf, why they should never give out their address, school name or telephone number on the Net, what sort of sites they can visit and what to do if they receive messages that make them uncomfortable. For some excellent practical advice on this subject, all parents should head off to Yahooligans at **http://www.yahooligans.com/docs/safety**.

If you're ever concerned about the Web sites your children might be visiting, remember that you can open Internet Explorer's **History** folder (located within your Windows directory) to see a list of all recently-accessed pages. For a clearer picture, click on **View | Details** and then **Last Visited** to sort by date and time.

Finally, there are two Internet services that are definitely not suitable places for children to visit without supervision: these are newsgroups and IRC chat channels. Many access providers refuse to carry certain newsgroups, such as the alt.sex and alt.binaries.pictures hierarchies, but articles in some quite innocent newsgroups may contain views or language you wouldn't want your kids to read. The same goes for IRC. As we mentioned in Chapter 8, many chat channels are sexual in nature, and often in name too. But the type of people trying to make contact with children through IRC won't limit themselves to those channels. If you have kids in the house, it's strongly recommended that you don't have an IRC program installed on your computer.

Is any type of chat safe for kids?

Online services' general chat rooms are moderated (controlled by a representative of the service) to keep things friendly – AOL are especially good in that department. If you access the net through an IAP, give your children a copy of PowWow For Kids (see Chapter 8).

Get a little extra help

If all this seems a bit too much to handle on your own, don't worry! There are many software programs around that can take over some of the supervision for you. To balance maximum access with maximum security, you need a program that can identify the actual content about to be viewed, rather than the name of the page or site. There are many such programs available, but here's a short list of the most respected:

▷ **Net Nanny** from
   http://www.netnanny.com/home.html

▷ **CYBERsitter** from
   http://www.solidoak.com/cysitter.htm

▷ **SurfWatch** from **http://www.surfwatch.com**

▷ **Cyber Patrol** from **http://www.cyberpatrol.com**

Some of these programs, such as Net Nanny, are especially powerful in that they don't work solely with Internet programs – they can bar access to documents viewed using any program on your computer. When your start your computer, Net Nanny runs invisibly in the background and watches for particular words or phrases. If they appear, Net Nanny instantly replaces them with X's, and threatens to shut down the program in 30 seconds unless you enter a valid password. The words in question may appear in email messages, Web pages or chat rooms, they may be in files on floppy disks or CD-ROMs or they may form the name of a file. You can add words, phrases, applications and Web sites to Net Nanny's list and download regularly-updated lists of restricted sites. For added parental reassurance, Net Nanny also keeps a note of any attempts to access restricted sites, as do many other programs.

NET TIP

Don't take these tools for granted

These 'babysitter' programs are useful tools, but a curious or technology-minded child might still find ways to override them. It isn't easy, but these are those same kids that remind us how to set the video-recorder!

Net Nanny says
'No!'

Is it safe to use my credit card on the Internet?

Another popular myth about the Internet is that credit card transactions are risky because your card number can be stolen. To put this in perspective, consider how you use your credit or debit card in the 'real world'. How many people get to see your card number during a normal week? How much time does your card spend out of your view when you use it? Do you always ask for the carbon paper after signing for a credit card purchase? The truth is, card numbers are easy to steal. It takes a lot more effort and technical know-how to steal numbers on the Internet.

Making the computer-hacker's job more difficult in this department, modern browsers can now encrypt the data they send, and most of the Web sites at which you can use your credit card run on secure servers that have their own built-in encryption. So when you visit one of these secure sites, enter your card number, and click the button to send it, your number will appear as meaningless gibberish to anyone managing to hack into the system. In fact, credit card companies actually regard online transactions as being the safest kind.

How can I tell when I visit a secure Web site?

In Internet Explorer, look for a little padlock symbol in the lower right corner of the browser. In Netscape's lower left corner you'll see a similar padlock which will be locked at secure sites and unlocked at the rest. You'll also notice that the http:// in the address bar changes to https://. More and more shopping sites are becoming secure all the time, and those that aren't usually offer alternative payment methods.

Cookies — are they safe to eat?

They sound cute and harmless, but what are they? Well, they're not particularly cute, but cookies are small text files that are stored on your computer's hard disk when you visit certain Web sites. To take a look at them, open your Windows directory, and then open the Cookies directory you find inside – you can double-click any of these cookies to read its contents in Notepad.

Cookies can serve several uses to the creator of a Web site, and some can even benefit visitors like you and me. A cookie might contain a unique code that identifies you, saving the need to enter a name and password when you visit, and perhaps allowing you to access restricted areas of a site. They're also often used by online shopping sites as a sort of 'supermarket trolley' that keeps track of the purchases you select until you're ready to pay and leave. Sites that rely heavily on displaying banner advertisements for their income might track 'click-throughs', keeping a log of the path you follow through the site and the pages you decide to visit. Knowing a bit about your interests in this way enables the site to target you with the type of adverts most likely to get your attention.

Do all cookies have practical uses?

No. You may visit a personal site that asks you to enter your name which it then stores in a cookie. On every future visit, you'll see a message like Hello John, you've visited this page four times. It's pointless, but it's still harmless.

So, are they safe? Yes, they are. Cookies are often misunderstood – they can't be used to read any other data from your hard disk, to find out what software you've got installed or to pass on personal information. When you visit a Web site, the page doesn't 'search' your hard disk for a cookie; instead, your browser sends the cookie containing the URL of the site as soon as you type in the address or click the link.

The wider question is whether you want anyone using your hard disk as a type of mini-database in this way – it's a point of principle rather than safety. If you want to join the anti-cookie ranks, Internet Explorer can help. Click on **View | Options | Advanced**, and check the box beside **Prompt before accepting "cookies"**. Every time a site tries to store a cookie on your disk you'll be given the choice of accepting or rejecting it. Be warned though – some sites just won't let you in if you won't eat the cookie! A more practical method is just to delete the entire contents of your Cookies directory as soon as you've finished surfing for the day.

How private is my email?

The words email and private don't go together well. Not that the world and his dog are going to read every message you send, of course, but email can get you into trouble (and people have got into very hot water through using email where a phone call or a quiet chat would have been wiser). If you're concerned about who could read it, don't write it.

The most obvious problem is that your 'private' messages can be easily forwarded or redirected, or the recipient might simply fail to delete an incriminating message after reading it. But apart from existing on your computer and the recipient's computer, however briefly, the message also spends time on your access provider's mail server and that of the recipient's access provider. Will the message really be deleted from both? And what if the administrator of one of these systems decides to run a backup while your message is waiting to be delivered?

If you really must use email to exchange sensitive messages, you might want to consider using **encryption** to scramble them. Messages are encrypted and decrypted using two codes called keys that you type into the encryption software. One is your private

---

 Need more encryption information?

The most popular encryption program is called PGP (Pretty Good Privacy). Although unbreakable, it isn't easy to use and you might want an extra program that sits on top and puts a 'friendlier face' on it. Go to **http://www.yahoo.com/Computers_and_Internet/ Security_and_Encryption** to learn more about the system and the software available.

key, the other is a public key that you'd hand out to anyone who needed to use it, or perhaps post on the Internet. If someone wanted to send you an encrypted message, they'd use your freely-available public key to encrypt it, and then send it off as usual. The message can only be decoded using your private key, and only you have access to that key. Likewise, if you wanted to send someone else a private message, you'd use his public key to encrypt it.

The Electronic Entertainment Guide

In This Chapter...

⇨ Use electronic TV and radio guides

⇨ See the latest movies, and book theatre tickets online

⇨ Find out what's on in towns and cities around the UK

⇨ Book hotels, holidays, flights and cars

⇨ Giggles, games and gambling online

I t's a paper world. It doesn't matter what you want to do, nine times out of ten you have to consult a piece of paper before you can do it. Want to watch TV? Book a holiday? See what's on at your local cinema or theatre? Plan a trip or a day out?

If you do any of those things, you've probably got a mountain of guides, catalogues, brochures and local newspapers, and many of them are probably out of date! So let's go paperless...

Use online TV & radio listings

No more scrabbling around to see which of those 28 Sunday supplements contains the TV listings this week – just hit the Web instead! Visit Events Online's TV page at **http://www.eventsonline.co.uk/cgi-eol/tv.cgi** for the fastest and most comprehensive guide to seven days of TV. Choose the five channels you want from the drop-down lists (or select **Ignore** if you want less than five), click the option button beside the appropriate day, and then click the **Get TV Listings** button. When the list appears, you can click on a programme's entry to see a brief description. And, of course, you can save the list to your own disk to read offline by selecting **File | Save As**.

Events Online is one of the UK's most popular sites – it's a sort of 'one-stop shop', so it can get pretty busy. If you can't connect, or it won't show you the listings, don't despair: head off to **http://www.link-it.com/tv**, where you'll find listings for peak-time viewing.

Where can I get satellite TV listings?

Visit the Satellite Times at **http://www.satellite-tv.co.uk** to find schedules for over 80 satellite channels available in the UK, plus features and reviews. Or check out Sky's own site at **http://www.sky.co.uk** and the Discovery Channel at **http://www.discovery.com**.

You'd expect Auntie Beeb to have her own Web site, and indeed she does. Point your browser at **http://www.bbc.co.uk/schedules/prog_by_day.html**, pick a day, and then choose a BBC TV channel or one of the BBC's five national radio stations for a complete programme listing, together with short descriptions. This is a huge site, and many popular BBC programmes have their own mini-sites within it. Head for **http://www.bbc.co.uk**, click on **UK Television** and select one of the categories such as Drama, Films, Entertainment or Natural History.

Need a few more TV and radio links?

▷ **http://www.dananeda.demon.co.uk/marklard**. A little lunacy from the Radio 1 afternoon stars.

▷ **http://www.ctw.org**. Despite the appalling title (Children's Television Workshop), this Sesame Street site brilliantly combines fun and education for young children, although a little parental help might be needed.

▷ **http://www.yahoo.co.uk/Regional/Countries/ United_Kingdom/News_and_Media/Radio/Stations**. Links to the Web sites of over 80 local radio stations.

▷ **http://www.channel4.com**. A well-designed and stylish site for Channel 4, complete with programme listings and an easy-to-navigate set of buttons.

NET TIP

Soap heaven

Need to catch up with your favourite UK soaps? Head for **http://www.geocities.com/TelevisionCity/2533** for the latest news and plot developments. You'll even find 'spoiler' pages of future plot lines here, but they're easily avoided if you prefer the suspense!

▷ *You don't necessarily need a radio to listen to the radio – this is the Internet after all; practically anything's possible. Skip ahead to Chapter 15 to find out more.*

Want to take in a movie?

The Web can tell you just about everything you want to know about movies and cinemas except for the price of the popcorn, and the site to check out is MovieWeb at **http://movieweb.com/movie/movie.html**. Here you'll find an alphabetical list of movies going back to 1995 with cast information and plot synopses, pictures and posters, and a lot more. MovieWeb gets previews of new movies long before they hit the cinema, and you can view these online in QuickTime format (you'll find out more about QuickTime in Chapter 15). And if you're not sure what's worth seeing, the weekly Top 25 box office charts should point you in the right direction.

Video previews of the latest movies at MovieWeb

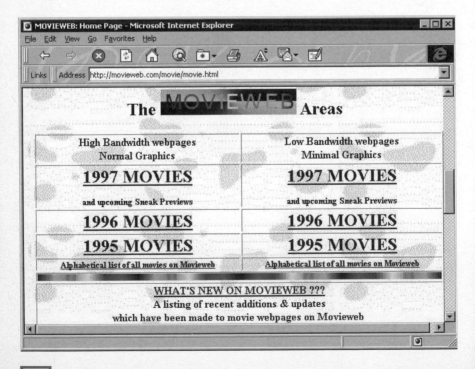

Once you've chosen the movie you'd like to see, it's time to find the local cinema showing it. To do that, head off to Yell's site at **http://www.yell.co.uk** and click the **Film Finder** link. Or maybe you were looking for older movies to buy on video? If so, get your credit card details ready and you may find what you want at The Zone, **http://www.thezone.co.uk**.

If you're a real movie addict, it's worth visiting the UK Internet Movie Database at **http://uk.imdb.com/a2z**. This site isn't as up-to-the-minute as MovieWeb and you won't find any previews here, but you will find quotes, reviews, news, and plenty of fun.

How about a night at the opera?

Or if opera's not to your taste, perhaps a ballet, an ice show, a pantomime, a kids show, or the latest Andrew Lloyd Webber musical. Make your way to What's On Stage at **http://www.whatson.com/stage** (shown in the next screenshot) and run a simple search for live entertainment in the area near you. You can select a single region or the whole of the UK, and choose one of 17 categories of stage-shows if you're looking for something in particular. You can even confine your search to particular dates, or use keywords.

 Finding more culture

UK Calling (at **http://www.uk-calling.co.uk/frame.html**) is a very attractive site with extensive listings in eight categories, including Classical Music, Art Galleries, Dance, Theatre, and Leisure Breaks. Or visit Events Online (**http://www.eventsonline.co.uk**) and click a category, or browse by event type or venue.

When you've found a show you'd like to see, you can usually book tickets online. Click the **Tickets** button, fill in the form, and you should receive email confirmation within three days.

---

stage at www.whatson.com - Microsoft Internet Explorer

File   Edit   View   Go   Favorites   Help

WHAT'S ON STAGE

TICKETS
BOOKS
MUSIC
INFO

≡ THIS WEEK ≡ LOCATION ≡ GENRE ≡ GREEN ROOM ≡ HOME ≡

The only *comprehensive* UK theatre listing service on the Web

THE LATEST

Last updated on **Fri 14th March 1997**

- There's a new club, **the Stage Musical Appreciation Society**, for all lovers of musicals. For more details and application forms contact them at SMASH, PO Box 148, Guildford GU1 2XU.

- Steven obviously enjoyed Miss Saigon on Monday, and let us know by Tuesday morning! *Hi, Just wanted to say thank you very much for last night. We enjoyed it immensely. It was the first*

KEYWORD SEARCH

Search using keywords :

[   ] GO

ALTERNATIVE SEARCH

Or browse the performances by selecting one or more of the location, date and/or genre categories below:

[South East   ▼]
[Stand-up Comedy   ▼]

Starting from this day:

[1   ▼] of: [February ▼]

Click on Location or Genre, or run a search for the best stage-shows

Get away for the weekend

If you're going to book up to see a show, why not make a weekend of it? The first thing you'll want to do is to find somewhere to stay, so wander over to Expotel at **http://www.expotel.co.uk**. You can choose between several search options such as a region of the UK, or the name of a hotel, or you can just click **Show me all the hotels in the UK** and then pick a town or city from the list to see what's available. Every hotel listing gives prices and facilities, and **First Choice** and **Second Choice** buttons: choose two hotels and set one as your first and one as your second choice, and then

---

✓ **NET TIP**

Insecure, but keen to help

The Expotel booking form isn't a secure site. If you don't want to enter your credit card details, you can send Expotel a fax instead, or just leave that section blank to have them phone you on receipt.

click the **Book hotel choices** button to fill in the online booking form.

If you can't find what you're looking for at Expotel, try visiting the UK Hotel & Guest House Directory at **http://www.s-h-systems.co.uk/shs.html**. This uses handy clickable maps to pinpoint a location (along with ordinary hypertext links for the geographically-challenged!), and gives all the important information about each hotel. Booking isn't quite as nifty here: you send an email which is delivered to the hotel as a fax, and they should then get in touch with you to confirm the details.

Where to go, what to do

So you've got tickets to a show, and booked a hotel, but what will you do with the rest of the weekend? Once again, the Web leaps in to help – try one of these sites:

▷ **Open World.** Over 800 heritage attractions, museums, theatres and restaurants, with clickable maps, plenty of pictures, and its own search engine. You can even search for accommodation based on price range! You'll find this at **http://www.openworld.co.uk/britain**.

▷ **UK Guide.** A smaller but growing site, sadly missing a search engine, but well worth clicking around. A much-needed Eating Out section should be online soon. Go to **http://www.uk-guide.com**.

▷ **Events Online.** A popular site, probably as much for its clarity and simplicity as its content. Click one of the friendly, coloured categories such as Music, Arts, Stage or Kids. You'll find this at **http://www.eventsonline.co.uk**.

And don't forget our old pal Yahoo! Point your browser at **http://www.yahoo.co.uk/Regional/Countries/United_Kingdom/Cities_and_Towns** for a list of hundreds of cities, towns and villages. The entries for a particular town can be a bit of a mixed bag – all types of local information may be listed here, from tourist attractions and restaurants to council offices and butchers. If you're looking for something particular, such as a zoo or a theme park, visit Yahoo's front page (**http://www.yahoo.co.uk**) and use a keyword search.

NET TIP

Want to play a round?

What better way to relax than to hit a little ball very hard and then go looking for it. If you're tired of looking in all the usual places, visit **http://www.golfweb.com/europe** and try a change of course.

Getting from A to B

Finally, let's sort out those travel arrangements. For this, there's one magical Web site that handles the lot – the UK Online All-In-One page, which you'll find at **http://www.ukonline.co.uk/UKOnline/Travel/contents .html**. From here, you can access dozens of European and international airlines and airports and check flight information; find the departure and arrival times of

A tiny slice of UK Online's incredible resource for travellers

UKOnline's All-In-One British Train, Airline... - Microsoft Internet Explorer

File Edit View Go Favorites Help

UK Airlines

British Airways

British Airways' online timetable is updated weekly and covers flights until 27 March 1998. It includes flights operated by British Airways as well as its Franchise and Codeshare Partner airlines and Deutsche BA and TAT. Note that this timetable only covers *direct* flights, it does not include routings that require a connection. Your query will show return as well as outbound flights if you tick the relevant box below. BA also provides online booking and ticket price information for flights from the UK.

Starting Country, Town, City, or Airport: **Destination:**

Depart Between: **And:**

01   Jan   01   Jan
1997   1997

Tick this box to be shown the times of return flights, too ☐

Search For Flight Times   Clear and Start Again

Virgin Atlantic

- Aer Lingus
- Air Malta
- Alitalia
- Austrian Airlines
- Czech Airlines
- Finnair
- Iberia
- KLM
- LOT Polish Airlines
- Lufthansa
- Luxair
- Ryanair
- Sabena
- SAS
- Swissair

OTHER INTERNATIONAL AIRLINES
- Aeroflot
- Air Canada
- Air New Zealand
- American
- Cathay Pacific
- Continental
- El Al

trains and National Express coaches; and book seats on planes, trains and buses. If that isn't enough, you can hire a car from one of four companies (or visit Hertz at **http://www.hertz.com/index.html**), check the latest news on motorways, London traffic and the tube, or look at the World Ski Report.

Book your holiday on the Web

If you want to journey further afield, the Internet has to be the ideal place to start. With a few clicks you can book flights and accommodation, read city guides, swot up on culture and currency, and check local events. You might even find a few photos that don't have painted blue skies! Here's some of the best sites:

▷ **Internet Travel Network** at **http://www.itn.net**. Enter itinerary details to check pricing and availability, book hotels and hire cars. Instead of entering your credit card number, choose a travel agent and you'll be contacted for the final reservation details.

▷ **World Travel Guide** at **http://travelguide.attistel.co.uk/start.html** Don't even consider going abroad without coming here first. Every useful piece of information you could ever need is on this site.

▷ **Thomas Cook** at **http://www.thomascook.com**. A mine of useful information including currency conversion, special offers, and links to other sites.

▷ **Eurostar** at **http://www.eurostar.com**. Fare and timetable information for passenger services through the Channel Tunnel, as well as online reservations.

▷ **Internet Travel Service** at **http://www.itsnet.co.uk**. Links to sites offering information about every aspect of travel you could imagine, including Health, Self-Catering, Insurance, Ferries, Cycling Holidays, Travel Agents… the list is almost endless.

To find general What's On? information in the major cities of the world, a couple of useful starting points are Excite's CityNet (**http://www.city.net**) and *Time Out* magazine (**http://www.timeout.co.uk**). The *Time Out* site requires you to register by entering your name, address, email address, and some extra fact-finding information.

NET TIP

Let's talk travel

Usenet is a useful source of travel information and real-life experiences. Check out the **alt.travel** and **rec.travel.marketplace** newsgroups, and take a look at the rest of the **rec.travel** hierarchy.

Amuse the kids (and yourself!) online

Once you've discovered the Web, you've got a whole new world of entertainment at your fingertips. The effort that people put into creating some of these sites is stunning, and they do it for no particular reward. There's no 'licence fee' to pay, and you won't get interrupted by advertisements every 15 minutes!

Entertainment sites for kids

The best children's sites are the ones that take a little education and add a sugar-coating of fun and interactivity, and America is leagues ahead of the UK in this department. In fact, UK kids' sites are thin on the ground, and good sites are probably still a year or two away. As long as you're not too concerned about the odd bit of weird spelling, point your kids at **http://www.yahooligans.com** for a mass of links to tried and trusted Web pages.

Of course, you may not be convinced that the Internet is a safe or worthwhile place for kids. Prepare to be persuaded! Fire up your browser and visit **http://www.bonus.com**, shown in the following screenshot. As soon as you arrive, the 'worthwhile'

element should be obvious: there are over 500
activities for kids, including games and puzzles,
animations, interactive adventures, scientific
explorations, and a whole lot more. The entire site is
colourful, stylish, and easy to navigate. But apart from
the incredible content you'll find here, this site
illustrates the sense of responsibility found increasingly
on the Web – your kids are locked in and they can't
escape! Whenever you visit this site, a second browser
window opens automatically, minus toolbars and
menus, to display the pages; your children can move
around this site to their hearts' content, but the only
way to access a different site is to return to the original
window and choose a Favorites item or type a URL
into the address bar.

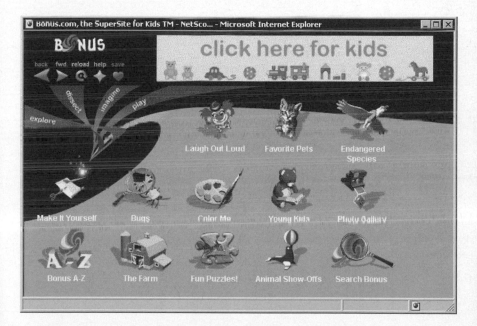

Another site that knows how to keep kids
entertained, not surprisingly, is Disney at
http://www.disney.co.uk. Although the content here is
clearly tilted towards the latest cinema and video
releases, there's no big sell. Instead, you'll find games

Bonus.com, a
truly absorbing
site on the Web.
But give your kids
a go too!

and activities that tie in cleverly with the films, with plenty of favourite cartoon characters, animated story-books, and a very friendly, 'kids-club' feel. You can also find out more about the various Disney resorts, and watch live-camera broadcasts from Main Street.

NET TIP

Spin a yarn for the Web

Do you have a budding novelist in the family? Point your kids at KidPub (**http://www.kidpub.org/kidpub**) where they can submit their own stories and read other children's creations online.

The sheer novelty value of surfing the Internet can be enough to keep kids amused for hours (if your phone bill can stand it!), and a particular branch of Web-based entertainment also makes a great starting point for learning how the Net works – the online scavenger hunt. Working from a set of clues, the goal is to track down pictures, pages and information on the Internet, like a treasure hunt at a kids' party. In fact, scavenger hunts are popular with adults too (especially the ones that pay cash prizes!), and often lead you to explore areas of the Internet that you'd studiously avoided. A current list of scavenger hunts can be found if you head off to **http://www.yahoo.co.uk/Entertainment/Contests__ Surveys__Polls/Scavenger_Hunts**

Play online games with other Web-surfers

If you like games, this is what you've been waiting for. Yahoo! offers 38 categories of online games at **http://www.yahoo.co.uk/Recreation/Games/Internet_ Games/Interactive_Web_Games**. Some of these are single-user games in which you play against the clock, solve a brain-teaser, or try to beat someone else's highest score; others are multi-user games in which you play against anyone else that happens to be visiting the same site at the same time.

Looking for single-user games?

Visit Karl Hörnell's site at **http://www.tdb.uu.se/~karl** for a collection of beautifully-crafted games including Mastermind, IceBlox, and RubikCube.

If you're stuck for somewhere to start, here are a few suggestions:

▷ **Gameshows** at **http://www.gameshows.com**. From the creator of the TV show *Jeopardy*, here are two nifty word games called 'Out Of Order' and 'Strike A Match'. Before you can play, a few files have to be installed on your disk (it happens automatically and only takes a minute or two), and you can then pit your wits against those of other visitors to the site.

▷ **Casino Royale** at **http://www.funscape.com**. If you like a gamble, visit this site and play poker, blackjack, roulette, slot machines and more. It really is a gamble, though – you can win real money, you can lose real money, and you'll have to pay a few dollars of real money to open an account before you start!

▷ **Entertainment & Games** at **http://tucows.cablelnet.net/fun95.html**. Tucows is an excellent source of Internet software, and this page will point you towards dozens of online games such as backgammon, chess, trivia quizzes, and arcade shoot-em-ups. Download the software from this page, and then follow the instructions to visit the Web sites where all the action takes place.

Gags & giggles galore
The World Wide Web has a seemingly endless store of joke pages, cartoons, comic strips and comedy sites. For instance, a great TV page called UK Laughter Links

(**http://www.netlink.co.uk/users/tucker/comedy/link. html**) is devoted entirely to comedy shows like *Men Behaving Badly* and *Fawlty Towers*. For reams and reams of jokes and humour links, try The Comedy Corner at **http://www.geocities.com/Eureka/2531** or the British Comedy Library which can be found at **http://homepages.enterprise.net/achwong/Comedy/in dex.html**.

If you're a cartoon fan, your first stop should be the 10 Laughs A Day site at **http://obryan.com/10Laughs**. As the name suggests, this site delivers ten new cartoons every day, following regular themes such as pets and business on Mondays, to politics and the depraved on Fridays. And, if you haven't spent all your money at Casino Royale, you can spend the remainder on a T-shirt or mug bearing your favourite cartoon.

Whatever flavour of humour it is that you prefer, you'll find another generous helping on Usenet. A couple of self-explanatory newsgroups are **alt.binaries.pictures.cartoons** and **rec.arts.comics.strips**, and there are many more lurking in the **rec.humor**, **alt.humor** and **alt.jokes** hierarchies.

Instant News & Current Affairs

In This Chapter...

▷ Daily news and weather on the Internet

▷ Track investment performance and personal finances

▷ Create your own personalised news pages

▷ Custom news stories sent straight to your desktop

▷ Party politics and government online

E verybody wants news of one sort or another. And, of course, there's plenty of it – it's being made all the time! But where traditional newspapers can print no more than two or three editions per day, Internet news services can be updated hour-by-hour, or even minute-by-minute.

In this chapter you'll find some of the best sources of UK and world news, learn how to build your own tailor-made news service, and meet the revolutionary Internet technology that's about to make your paperboy redundant.

Read your newspaper on the Web

Unexpectedly, it's the broadsheets that have made it to the Internet first, and they've made a surprisingly good job of combining content, style, and usability. If you find the paper versions of *The Times* and the *Daily Telegraph* a bit stuffy, their online versions are going to come as a revelation.

Let's take *The Times* (at **http://www.the-times.co.uk**) as an example. As soon as you arrive at the site's front page you're faced with clear icons that take you to *The Times* 'newspaper' itself, *The Sunday Times,* the Education supplements, and the Interactive Times. The latest news stories are easy to find: selecting the link to *The Times* presents summaries of the major stories in several categories, with hypertext links to the related articles if you'd like more detail, plus TV and weather. In true newspaper style, you'll also find links to classified ads, cartoons, crosswords and puzzles, and more hypertext-linked news summaries by visiting the Interactive Times.

So, it's all there, and it's easy to navigate. But what makes it better than an ordinary paper version? In a word – storage! Both *The Times* and the electronic Telegraph (at **http://www.telegraph.co.uk**), are building ever-expanding databases of news articles. With a quick keyword search, you can retrace the path of a news story you missed, track down articles on a particular subject, or find out what made headline news on any particular day.

Information swapping

Although access is usually free, when you first visit many online newspapers and magazines, you'll have to fill in one of those infamous registration forms, giving your name and address, and a few other details. This provides useful marketing information for the publishers which they regard as a fair exchange for the information they're giving you.

Let's talk about the weather

The weather is officially the most popular topic of conversation in the UK. And the Internet has a solution to that centuries-old problem, what can you do when there's no-one around to listen? Just start up your newsreader and head for **alt.talk.weather** or **uk.sci.weather**.

To become a real authority on the subject, however, you need to know what the weather is going to do next. One option is to consult the online newspapers mentioned above, but here's a better one: head for **http://weather.yahoo.com/Regional/United_Kingdom.html**. On this page, you'll find a hypertext list of almost every town in the UK – click on the appropriate town to see a five-day local weather forecast. (You might want to add the forecast page to Internet Explorer's **Favorites** menu or create a shortcut to it on your desktop for quick access.)

You will meet a tall dark stranger

Yes, the Net has horoscopes too! One of the best known is Jonathon Cainer's Zodiac Forecasts which can be found at **http://www.bubble.com/webstars/main.htm**. Or, for a more humorous approach, why not try visiting **http://www.xmission.com/ ~ mustard/cosmo.html**.

If you want more detailed weather information, including shipping forecasts and meteorological data, visit the Met Office site at **http://www.meto.govt.uk/sec3/sec3.html**.

Play the money markets online

There's little that can't be done on the Internet, but a few things cost money, and share dealing is one of them. Because the sort of information you're looking for is worth money, you'll have to whip out your credit card and cross palms with silver before you can trade. Nevertheless, there's no shortage of companies on the Internet holding their palms out expectantly, and one of the better known is Electronic Share Information (ESI) at **http://www.esi.co.uk**. Alternatively, nip along to The Share Centre at **http://www.share.co.uk** – this is a good, easy-to-follow site for new investors, offering plenty of straightforward help and explanations of the financial world. (Oddly, you can buy classical music CDs here too!)

MoneyWorld makes an excellent starting place for all things financial

For information on more wide-ranging money matters, the place to be is definitely MoneyWorld (**http://www.moneyworld.co.uk**). This is a huge and popular site covering every aspect of personal finance

you can imagine – homebuying and mortgages, PEPs, unit and investment trusts, and company performance, to name but a few. You can read the London closing business report, check the FTSE 100 and 250, view regularly updated world prices, and consult the glossary to find out what everyone's talking about. And if MoneyWorld doesn't have the information you're looking for, you'll find links to other financial services and organisations in the UK and abroad.

Money talks

NET TIP

Usenet has several newsgroups for people wanting to give or receive financial advice. A good starting point is **uk.finance**. For more international input, try **misc.invest** and **misc.invest.stocks**, and have a look at the **clari.biz.stocks** hierarchy.

Online newspapers such as the Electronic Telegraph, mentioned earlier in this chapter, also provide city news and prices just like their disposable counterparts, but if you need in-depth analysis, you can find the major finance publications on the Web too:

▷ *The Financial Times* at **http://www.ft.com**.

▷ *The Wall Street Journal* at **http://www.wsj.com**.

▷ *The Economist* at **http://www.economist.com**.

Financial scandals

NET TIP

The financial world has caught a few hands in a few tills in recent years. To find out more about financial scandals and the owners of those unfortunate hands, hurry along to **http://www.ex.ac.uk/ ~ RDavies/arian/scandals.htm**.

Create your own custom news page

You may well buy a newspaper every day, and perhaps a weekly or monthly trade journal of some sort. But do you actually read them all from cover to cover? The chances are that you glance at the headlines or the contents page, read the articles that interest you, and ignore the rest. Wouldn't it be great if there was one publication you could buy that gave you just the stories that appealed to you and left out everything else? Well there is. In fact, there are quite a few, and you don't even have to pay for them!

The 'personal page' is a recent arrival to the Web, but more and more online publications are building the option into their sites. If you find a trade journal that covers one of your hobbies or interests, take a look around the site to see if it offers the service, or send an email to ask if it's in the pipeline.

NET TIP

The best of Times

The Times Internet Edition lets you create a personal news page by choosing the types of business, arts, national and world news that interest you. Click the Interactive Times icon, then Personal Times, and check the boxes to specify your preferences.

Latest news, delivered straight to your desktop!

In the busy hurly-burly of modern life, the personal news page is a great time saver, but you still have to visit the Web site to read it. By today's technological standards, that's much too inconvenient. Instead, the news should come to you, and it should do so without even being asked.

The latest Internet innovation is **push technology**, a system that's expected to be at the heart of future Net development. In a nutshell, any type of information you could find on the Web can be sent straight to your desktop – text, pictures, sounds, video, and more – without the need for surfing and searching. You simply install the software, set a few preferences, and then sit back and watch as your personalised content streams down the line to you. And, although the technology is in its infancy, you can already receive regularly-updated world news, sports results, weather, share prices, and leisure information.

Push technology

This is also known as server push. Instead of your computer 'pulling' the information from the Web when you ask for it (client pull), the Web literally 'pushes' the information down the line to you and keeps it updated automatically.

The main program on everyone's lips for personalised news is called the PointCast Network (shown in the next screenshot), and you can download it free from **http://www.pointcast.com**. Its main drawback, at the time of writing, is its heavily American content, but the company is working hard at

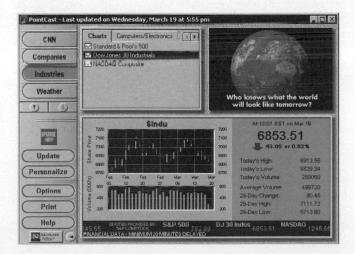

Dynamic news on your desktop, courtesy of the PointCast Network

providing localised coverage. Getting up and running with PointCast is quick and easy – just follow these steps:

1 After you've installed the software, click the **Personalize PointCast** button that appears, and fill in a few personal details. You'll also have to select the method you use to connect to the Internet.

2 Next, you'll see a set of tabbed pages. These are PointCast's channels, following a television metaphor. On the first page you can select up to eight channels to follow from a list of categories such as news, weather, sports and lifestyle. Clicking the other tabs lets you fine-tune the content to be included in each channel.

3 Finally, click **OK**, and PointCast will automatically download and display the information you selected. You can move between channels using the buttons on the left of the screen, and click on tabs and stories to view them on the right.

NET TIP

Internet Explorer's channels

Internet Explorer has its own set of channels that include Business, Entertainment, Sports and News. Click the Channels button on the toolbar and follow the instructions to audition and subscribe to the channels that interest you.

You can change the content to be downloaded, and add or remove channels, any time you want to by clicking the **Personalize** button to return to those tabbed pages. Selecting the **Options** button lets you choose whether PointCast should dial-up and retrieve information automatically at regular intervals: you can set the frequency of these updates, or (as a more practical method for UK users) bypass the automation and just click **Update** when you want to download the latest batch of news. By default, PointCast also sets itself as your screensaver – if you haven't read the Help file this could come as a bit of a shock, especially if you don't know how to override it!

All-in-one news & weather

NET TIP

If you prefer to find your news, weather and sports information all in one place, go to **http://www.yahoo.co.uk/headlines** and choose news headlines or summaries in several categories, together with UK, Irish and world-wide weather forecasts.

Chart hits & bestsellers

If you're interested in the music charts visit Dotmusic, at **http://www.dotmusic.co.uk**, one of the most successful UK music sites on the Web. Along with the albums and singles charts and other information about the music scene, you'll find the Indie singles and albums charts, dance, R & B and club charts, and the US Airplay chart. While you're there, watch out for the little basket icons – if a CD you want to buy has one of these symbols beside it, you can click to add it to your 'shopping basket', and pay at the checkout when you're ready to leave. You'll need to enter a valid credit or debit card number, but Dotmusic is a secure site (see page 154) and its payment routine is easy to follow.

Your bank account isn't running the same risks at the Publishers Weekly Bestseller Lists (**http://www.bookwire.com/PW/bsl/bestseller-index.html**), but you'll find useful lists of the current bestsellers sorted by hardback and paperback fiction or non-fiction, children's, religious, computer, and audio books. For more general information and reviews, the main Bookwire site makes an ideal starting point – head for the homepage at **http://www.bookwire.com**.

Politics & politicians on the Internet

Whether you want to explore 10 Downing Street, delve into government archives, read press releases and speeches, or check electoral and constituency information, the Internet has all the resources you need. But let's start with the obvious – if you're interested in politics, the first place you'll want to visit is your own party's Web site, so pay them a visit.

Political party	Web site URL
The Conservative Party	http://www.conservative-party.org.uk
The Green Party	http://www.gn.apc.org/greenparty
The Labour Party	http://www.labour.org.uk
The Liberal Democratic Party	http://www.libdems.org.uk
The Monster Raving Loony Party	http://www.raving-loony.pv.org
Plaid Cymru	http://www.wales.com/political-party/plaid-cymru/englishindex.html
The Scottish National Party	http://www.snp.org.uk

If you're more interested in the real workings of government, head for the Government Information Office at **http://www.open.gov.uk**. This is a huge site containing thousands of documents and articles, but there are several choices of index to help you find your way through it. The easiest method is probably to click on Functional Index and scroll through the alphabetical list looking for keywords relating to the subjects you want. Another well-organised and informative site is the Central Office of Information at **http://www.coi.gov.uk/coi/depts/deptlist.html**, which provides a comprehensive hypertext list of the many government departments on the Web.

Until recently, one of the few ways to get a look around 10 Downing Street was to become a politician – rather a high price to pay when one look is probably enough. Thanks to the wonders of the Web, you can enjoy tramping around to your heart's content at **http://www.number-10.gov.uk**, and read a selection of speeches, interviews and press releases while you're there. Or you can even jump on a virtual bus to **http://www.parliament.uk** to tour the House of Commons and the House of Lords, and search through the parliamentary archives. Another revealing site is the Register of MPs' Interests, published by the *Guardian* (**http://www.guardian.co.uk/ interests/index.html**), which includes a search engine and some interesting commentary.

NET TIP

An Eye on the Net

You don't have to take politics entirely seriously, of course. For a more satirical view try that infamous establishment-knocker *Private Eye* at **http://www.compulink.co.uk/ ~ private-eye** or *Scallywag* at **http://www.xs4all.nl/ ~ emags/scallywag/index.html**.

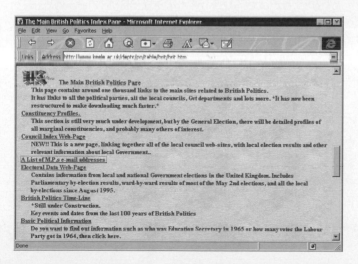

A huge resource of local and national political data at the Main British Politics Page

For all the government departments and official bodies on the Web, one of the most useful and informative sites is actually unofficial. The Main British Politics Page (**http://www.ukpol.co.uk**), shown in the screenshot on the previous page, is a veritable goldmine that includes local and national electoral information, constituency lists and analyses, local government details, and a useful Basic Information section. There are even lists of MPs' personal Web pages and email addresses.

Oil the wheels of government yourself!

Getting your voice heard in the crowd isn't easy, but if you can find a few people who share your views you can improve your chances. Or perhaps you'd like to let off a bit of steam, or get into a good old political scrap once in a while. The newsgroups provide one of the few resources available anywhere that allow you to discuss your political opinions with people from all over the world. Indeed, they could even act as a springboard for launching pressure groups and petitions, or organising online 'conferences' using programs like NetMeeting and PowWow. The three major political newsgroups in the UK are **alt.politics.british**, **alt.politics.europe.misc** and **uk.gov.local**, but you'll find many more under the **uk.politics** hierarchy. Or try filtering your list of groups by entering **politic** to find related groups in other Usenet hierarchies.

As an alternative to the newsgroups, a recent newcomer to the Web is UK Citizens Online

Why don't UK politicians answer questions?

They've probably learnt a lesson or two from the famously foot-in-mouth US Senator Dan Quayle! As a dose of light relief from everyday politics, read The 'Wisdom' of Dan Quayle at **http://www.concentric.net/ ~ salisar/quayle.html**.

Democracy at **http://www.democracy.org.uk**. This is a discussion site that works in a very similar way to the Usenet groups: you can post your own messages by email, and follow discussion threads by clicking on hypertext links. The major difference between this site and the political newsgroups is that UK politicians actually take part in the discussions. In the words of the site itself: 'We hope it will become a place to make things happen – an exciting new interface between the public and politicians.'

Learning & Working with the Internet

In This Chapter...

▷ Online schools, universities and study tools

▷ Use dictionaries, encyclopaedias, quotations and more

▷ Locate online maps, atlases and city guides

▷ Find pictures, videos and information about the entire universe

▷ How the Internet can help you find a job

Whatever you do in your daily life, the Internet can help. It can provide you with vital reference and study materials; enable you to work or study from home; and put you in touch with other users working in a similar field.

And if your daily life leaves you too much time for aimless surfing, the Internet can even help you find a job!

Schools & educational sites

Education is at an interesting stage in its online development. Although universities and colleges were among the first sites to appear on the Net, online classes are still few and far between. The technology is there: conferencing programs like NetMeeting can link students to classes using video and sound; course-work can be sent back and forth by email; reference materials can be read from the World Wide Web.

One of the few UK organisations that can provide courses over the Internet is the Open University. Their site, at **http://www.open.ac.uk**, explains how the system works, and they'll even provide you with the software you need. There are details of all the available courses here, and you can apply for a place on a course by email.

The tradition for universities and colleges to have a presence on the Internet hasn't abated, and you can track them all down easily from the clickable maps at **http://scitsc.wlv.ac.uk/ukinfo/uk.map.html**. This page

 NET TIP

Schools on the Web

ifl@school (at **http://www.rmplc.co.uk**) is a site dedicated to UK schools on the Internet, with national curriculum information, a noticeboard and a penpals page. It also features EduWeb, a list of email addresses and Web page links to thousands of schools nationwide.

shows universities, and two links at the top of the page open similar maps for UK colleges and research establishments – click on any location and you'll be whisked straight to its Web page. The links to research venues, especially, are many and varied, including museums, libraries and observatories, and make excellent resources for your own online research. The university sites have an extra value you might not think of straight away – many of them include a fund of local information such as bus and train timetables, maps, and places of interest.

Elsewhere on the UK Net, practical education sites are still very thin on the ground. One site that appeared relatively recently is GCSE Answers at **http://www.gcse.com**, giving exam information, tips for success, and summaries of syllabuses. At the time of writing, only Maths syllabuses and English language and literature are covered, but a few more should follow soon.

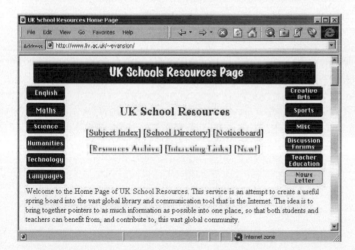

UK Schools Resources Page – an expanding education and reference site

For a wider array of curricular subjects, there are two excellent sites providing ready-sorted links to the best sites for Humanities, Sciences, Arts and general reference. The first is The Internet Educational Resources Guide which can be found at http://www.aber.ac.uk/ ~ magwww/reslist.html. This also allows keyword searches in each subject. Second is the UK Schools Resources Page; head off to http://www.liv.ac.uk/ ~ evansjon, shown in the previous screenshot. For schools, teaching professionals, and anyone wanting access to the best learning and study materials available, BT's CampusWorld is the place to be. You can find out more about this subscription service if you head off to http://www.campus.bt.com/CampusWorld.

Look it up online

You probably won't be using 'lookup' references on the Internet a great deal. In the UK, where a local phone call still costs money, going online every time you need to check the spelling of a word or find a synonym is hardly an economical pastime. More than likely, your word-processor has a built-in spellchecker and thesaurus; you may have a CD-ROM-based multimedia encyclopaedia too. But it's a safe bet that the Internet outweighs your book and CD-ROM collections, so here are some of the resources you can call on when you need to.

NET TIP

Material gains

If you need more reference materials than those given here and on the accompanying CD-ROM, point your browser at http://www.yahoo.co.uk/Reference for the characteristically comprehensive set of categories.

Encyclopaedias

The words 'online encyclopaedia' sound a bit odd. After all, the Internet itself is the ultimate encyclopaedia, so why would you search its contents for a smaller version? A search engine will provide a greater number and variety of links to information than any encyclopaedia. So the only time you're likely to want an online encyclopaedia is when you need concise, comprehensive information on a subject fast, and the only real contender is the *Encyclopaedia Britannica's* online incarnation at **http://www.eb.com**.

The Britannica site itself is excellent – you'll find an Image Tour, a word game, Random Article feature, news and current events articles, Birthday Lookup, and masses more. As for the reason you visited in the first place, the search facilities are fast and powerful: you can enter a keyword or phrase, or even type a question in standard English. The search engine will then give you the information intelligently – if it believes it's answered your question, it will display the relevant article, or the portion of an article that seems to contain the answer. As with keyword searches, you'll also find more links to related articles to help you dig deeper.

Being unique, Britannica is a subscription service. It comes at a price not far removed from that of your entire Internet access: $8.50 per month, or $85 per year. You can sign up for a seven-day trial by clicking the **Free Trial** icon, but be prepared for a rather convoluted registration process.

Kids encyclopaedia

Kids and teenagers can find a very good reference site at **http://www.adventure.com/library/encyclopedia**. This encyclopaedia allows keyword searches, browsing through its nine categories, or a trawl through its entire list of entries. Although it's a US site with an American slant, the information is well-presented and might make all the difference to school projects.

Dictionaries

How anyone finds the time to put them there is a mystery, but dictionaries of all types abound on the Internet. One of the best spelling and definition lookups is Webster's (subtly retitled WWWebster's for the Web) at **http://www.m-w.com/netdict.htm**. As usual, enter a keyword, and its pronunciation and definition will appear. If you're not sure of the spelling, just get as close as you can – WWWebster's will suggest some alternatives if it doesn't recognise your word. A great all-rounder is the OneLook Dictionaries site at **http://www.onelook.com**. This handy resource can search through 97 dictionaries simultaneously, or you can restrict your search to a particular area such as medical, computer-related, or religious dictionaries. Both WWWebster's and OneLook support the use of wildcards, allowing you to find multiple words or hedge your bets on the spelling.

Wildcards

Wildcards are characters used to represent unknown characters in a word. The asterisk replaces multiple letters (so you could enter demo* to find 'democracy' and 'demographic'); the question mark replaces a single letter (so te?t? would find 'tests' and 'teeth').

Dictionaries of every imaginable type at OneLook

OneLook Dictionaries, The Faster Finder - Microsoft Internet Explorer

File   Edit   View   Go   Favorites   Help

OneLook Dictionaries
The Faster Finder

(636438 words in 97 dictionaries now indexed)

Survey Results ||| Please answer survey, How do you say "FAQ" ||| Help Improve Literacy

Search For a Word in a Dictionary/Glossary on the Internet
Enter word: [   ]   LOOK IT UP

HINTS: Adding an asterisk wildcard in the word/term expands the dictionary/glossary search. For example, either "tomo*ow" or "tomor*" will find "tomorrow". You may limit the initial dictionary/glossary search by selecting specific dictionaries/glossaries below. A search is automatically expanded, if no match for the word/term is found.

1. Computer/Internet Dictionaries [   ]
2. Science Dictionaries [   ]
3. Medical Dictionaries [   ]
4. Technological Dictionaries [   ]
5. Business Dictionaries [   ]
6. Sports Dictionaries [   ]
7. Religion Dictionaries [   ]
8. Miscellaneous Dictionaries [   ]
9. Acronym Dictionaries [   ]
10. General Dictionaries [   ]

LOOK IT UP

Of course, neither of the above sites can help you much when you receive an email from your Hungarian penpal. For that you need a dual-language dictionary, and Dictionaries On The Web which can be found at **http://www.ling.helsinki.fi/~hkantola/dict.html** is the place to find one. This page contains links to a huge number of translating dictionaries including Russian, Estonian, Czech, Latin, and German, most of which translate to or from English and respond to the usual keyword input.

Quotations

'The Internet is a great way to get on the Net.' So sayeth US Senator Bob Dole, and it takes a brave man to disagree. Another good way is to say something sufficiently wise, amusing, or obtuse that people will include it in their online quotation pages. Everyone from Shakespeare to Stallone has said something quotable, and the best place to find it is at **http://www.geocities.com/Athens/Forum/1327**. This page gives an immense hypertext list of words from 'Ability' to 'Zest' - just click a likely word to open a page of related quotes.

Alternatively, visit Project Bartleby at **http://www.columbia.edu/acis/bartleby/bartlett** to read quotes by choosing an author from the list, or by running a keyword search. The quotes are limited to classical literature (no Oscar Wildes or George Bernard Shaws here), and the search engine responds best to a single-word entry.

NET TIP

Still no rhyme for 'orange'

The word 'orange' continues to look an unlikely candidate for your latest love-poem, as confirmed by the Rhyming Dictionary at **http://www.cs.cmu.edu/~dougb/rhyme.html**. This keyword search lets you choose between perfect and partial rhymes, or homophones (such as there/their/they're).

And lots more besides...

Need to find the meaning of some of those acronyms and abbreviations that seem to crop up so often in modern life? Head off to the Acronym Lookup at **http://www.ucc.ie/cgi-bin/acronym**. This simple service consists of just a text box (nope, no button!). Type in your acronym, and press Enter to see the results.

Another often-needed reference is a weights and measures converter. To get a straightforward list of units and their conversion factors, you can visit **http://www.soton.ac.uk/ ~ scp93ch/refer/convfact.html**. The list is comprehensive, and appears on a single page, so you could even save the page to your own disk for easy use. But if you'd prefer to avoid the brain-exercise of doing the maths yourself, the Measurement Converter at **http://www.mplik.ru/ ~ sg/transl** has the answer. Choose one of the nine categories (such as Weight, Speed, Pressure or Area), type a figure in the appropriate box, and press the Tab key to see the equivalent value instantly displayed for all the other unit types.

Along similar lines, you'll find a useful currency converter at **http://www.xe.net/currency**. Type an amount into the text box, select your Convert From and Convert To currencies from the drop-down lists, and click the button to see the result based on the latest exchange rates.

Finally, here's an unusual cross between a search engine and a reference lookup. Wired Source (at **http://www.wired.com/cybrarian**) gives a list of categories such as Business, Companies, Politics, Science and Film. Choose one of these, and a page will open displaying a list of specialist search engines, sites and links, as shown in the next screenshot. Just pick the most likely-looking candidate on the page and submit a keyword search. Although it's an American site, and so some categories may not be helpful to UK users, this is one of the surest ways to find anything, from details of a patent application to the complete David Bowie discography.

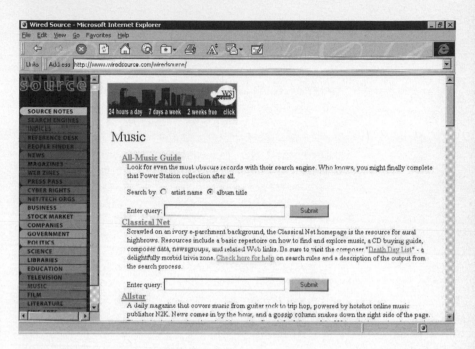

The Earth unearthed

When it comes to global or universal information, the potential for acquiring knowledge is inexhaustible. Whether you're looking for fact, conjecture or opinion, the Internet can help you find a street-map of Dallas, the best restaurant in Prague, a video of a lunar eclipse or several answers to the mystery of crop circles.

Wired Source gathers hundreds of search facilities into one easy-to-use site

Discover the world

There's no single, comprehensive site for maps and atlases, so if you want something in particular you'll have to be prepared for a bit of traipsing around. A good place to start, though, is Encyberpedia's map links at **http://www.encyberpedia.com/maps.htm**. Although the USA is disproportionately well-served, you'll also find maps of cities elsewhere in the world, atlases and historical maps, plus a few links to interactive and virtual reality map sites.

If you want some background information to go with your maps, try visiting the Excite search engine's

CityNet site at **http://city.net**. You can type the name of a country, region or city to run a keyword search, or (more enjoyably) click your way through the interactive maps to home in on the area you want. Once again, American cities are plotted and detailed to the last manhole cover at the expense of other countries, but it still manages to be a smart and informative site. If you like these clickable maps, you'll enjoy a visit to the superb graphics of Magellan Geographix at **http://www.magellangeo.com/HTML/atlas.html**.

For historical maps, visit the Oxford University Map Room at **http://rsl.ox.ac.uk/nnj**. You will also be able to find the Ordnance Survey online at two sites: **http://www.ordsvy.gov.uk** is the official government site, or, alternatively, **http://www.campus.bt.com/ CampusWorld/pub/OS/mainmenu.html** is an educational site giving examples, a key to OS symbols, and a UK gazetteer.

NET TIP

Flying colours

Looking for flags of the world? Why not head off to **http://flags.cesi.it/flags/allpaget.html** and click the flag you want from the list. The flags can be downloaded as GIF image files, and each is accompanied by a page of fascinating historical background.

Zooming out for a global view, there's a mass of information available. If you need to check up on a time zone in a hurry, you can head along to **http://tycho.usno.navy.mil/tzones.html**, a US Navy site, and click the initial letter of the country you're interested in. For a slower, but stylishly interactive, way of reaching similar information, the WorldTime site at **http://www.worldtime.com/cgibin/user/hb1005/wt.cgi** will keep you clicking around in fascination for ages as you zoom in and out, and switch between night and day.

The world in pictures

NET TIP

For the best images and movies of the Earth, visit the Earth Image Index at **http://bang.lanl.gov/solarsys/raw/earth**. This is a plain list of files (some quite large) in four categories: Animations, Earth Images, Earth Cloud Images, and Earth Impact Craters. Many files have accompanying text documents providing background information.

Understand the world

Why do we have seasons? What causes volcanoes and tornadoes? What is a rainbow? Even those of us who've been living on it for several decades still have questions about the Earth. As usual, the Web is the place to turn to find the answers, and it has one huge benefit over any encyclopaedia – if you can't find the explanation you're looking for, you can just ask!

One of the best 'question-and-answer' sites is ScienceNet, at **http://www.campus.bt.com**

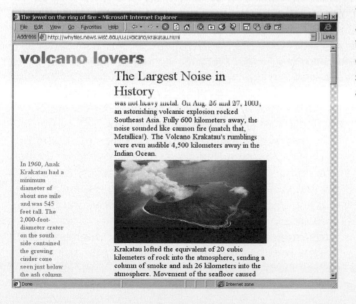

The Why Files – an easy and light-hearted collection of scientific answers

/CampusWorld/pub/ScienceNet/first.html. Here you'll find an immense database of questions in categories like Earth Science, Archaeology, Astronomy and Chemistry. The answers are clear, concise and non-technical, and you'll probably find yourself browsing through each category in fascination, but if you're looking for a particular answer you can run a keyword search or submit your own question by filling in a simple form and receive a reply by email.

A similar site, aimed more at children, is The Why Files at **http://whyfiles.news.wisc.edu**, shown in the screenshot above. Although there's no option to submit your own questions at the moment, the subjects covered are well chosen, with plenty of pictures, tasty facts you can impress your friends with, and a light-hearted approach.

New Horizons, Old Horizons

The BBC's popular series, Horizon, has a useful site at **http://www.bbc.co.uk/horizon**. As well as details of forthcoming programs, an Archive section collects many past documentaries into eight categories, with summaries of each. You can even download complete program transcripts.

One of the most popular questions, of course, is How did it all start?, and the Cosmic Web Site at **http://www.geocities.com/CapeCanaveral/Lab/2048** sets out to explain the popular Big Bang Theory for the creation of the universe. (Big Bang theorists haven't got the field to themselves though - maybe there was nothing there to go Bang in the first place, a point put forward by The Theory of Nothing at **http://members.aol.com/aambury/nothingness.html**.)

For general science-related features and articles, two of the best-known names are New Scientist magazine (**http://www.newscientist.com**) and the

BBC's Tomorrow's World (**http://www.bbc.co.uk/tw**). Both sites change regularly and hold large archives of past features, making them well worth visiting for general interest or for serious research.

New Scientist online: in-depth stories, a huge archive and easy searching

But if you prefer your science to be a little on the 'weird' side, head for **http://www.csltimo.com/~billb/ weird/wpage.html**. This links page will take you to stories about science hoaxes, jokes, unusual theories and much more in a similar vein, along with 'The Official Truth', a great collection of science-related quotations such as 'I think there is a world market for maybe five computers' from a past president of IBM.

Change the world

There are thousands of pressure groups and organisations dedicated to educating and improving the world, and you'll find many of them online. If you know the name of a particular organisation or society, try entering it into your favourite search engine; if you don't, enter descriptive keywords such as **wildlife protection**. Here are a few organisations you might want to visit:

Organisation	Web site URL
Amnesty International	http://www.oneworld.org/amnesty/index.html
Crime Prevention Initiative	http://www.crime-prevention.org.uk
Friends Of The Earth	http://www.foe.co.uk
Greenpeace International	http://www.greenpeace.org
Save The Children	http://www.oneworld.org/scf

The universe... and beyond!

If you need information about the rest of our solar system, the obvious starting point is NASA. In fact, the primary NASA site at **http://www.nasa.gov** is so immense it's hard to believe you'll ever need another site! Alongside image and movie galleries, there are sound files, details of new and current missions, information about the technology involved, the history of space travel and the NASA organisation itself.

If you want to find undiluted Shuttle information, go to **http://shuttle.nasa.gov**. This is an in-depth, but friendly, NASA site about Shuttle life, with videos of the craft taken from both inside and out, latest news about the Shuttle programme and a wealth of fascinating information that you won't find anywhere else.

To boldly go where no man has gone before, why not head for the Royal Greenwich Observatory at **http://www.ast.cam.ac.uk**. The site itself is unin-spiring, but its links can lead you to pictures from the Hubble Space Telescope and many more observatories around the world (some of which provide live camera feeds to the Web from their telescopes).

A popular topic of discussion on the Internet, as elsewhere, concerns the existence of little green men (and women, presumably) from outer space, and many Web sites and newsgroups have sprung up to present, discuss and dispute the evidence for UFOs. The best of these is The Quest, at **http://www.netfeed.com/**

pstevens/quest2.htm, which also covers crop circles, ancient civilisations, paranormal phenomena and many more mysteries and unanswered questions. Confirmed UFO addicts will want to visit Bufora, the British UFO Research Organisation, at **http://www.bufora.org.uk**, and the SETI Institute at **http://www.seti-inst.edu**.

Visit NASA, and you'll probably never be seen again!

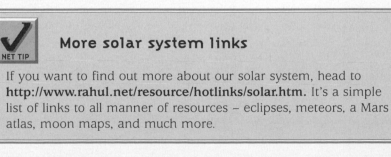

More solar system links

If you want to find out more about our solar system, head to **http://www.rahul.net/resource/hotlinks/solar.htm**. It's a simple list of links to all manner of resources – eclipses, meteors, a Mars atlas, moon maps, and much more.

Usenet, as usual, can put you in touch with other people around the world interested in the known and unknown universe. Take a look at the **sci.space** and **sci.astro** hierarchies, or drop in at **alt.sci.planetary**. You'll also find an **alt.paranormal** hierarchy, and there's a scattering of UFO-related groups that you can track down by filtering your newsgroups list with **ufo** (see page 106).

Find a job online

We all get involved in the employment market at some time in our lives, and it's usually a frustrating, hit-and-miss ordeal. Although the Internet can't give you any firm guarantees, it can give you access to resources that your 'unwired' competitors don't have, and it puts all of these right on your computer desktop to take a little of the drudgery out of job-searching and self-promotion.

Where can I learn to write a résumé?

Go to **http://www.yahoo.co.uk** and run a keyword search for **resume**. You'll see a list of Yahoo! employment categories that have a Resumes subcategory (click on **Next 20** to view more of the list). Pick a link that matches the type of work you're involved in, and browse through some of the résumés written by others to pick up a few ideas.

If you're looking for (or offering) full or part-time work, there are two UK sites which, between them, offer many thousands of vacancies. PeopleBank, at **http://www.peoplebank.com**, gives its services free to jobseekers. Fill in the online registration form, and submit your résumé or browse through the database of job vacancies. WorkWeb (**http://www.workweb.co.uk**) splits its vacancies into 25 searchable categories, and also provides support services for jobseekers and information about employment agencies.

If there's a particular company you'd like to work for, it's worth visiting their Web site. Many companies list their job vacancies online (although it sometimes takes a bit of clicking around to find the right page), and you can usually submit an application and CV by email. If you don't know the company's Web address, use your favourite search engine to search for the company name, or try **www.*company-name*.co.uk** or **www.*company-name*.com**.

Scan the professional journals

Yahoo! lists 15 categories of trade and professional journal such as Science, Culture, Computers and Arts. Head off to **http://www.yahoo.co.uk/Reference/Journals**, pick a suitable category and choose a journal to read online.

If you want to be even more enterprising, why not publish your résumé on the World Wide Web for all to see? If your line of work involves something that can be demonstrated on a computer, such as graphic design, journalism, or music, you could even include examples on your Web site. Most IAPs and online services provide free Web space, and in Chapter 16 you'll learn how to go about creating your pages.

Newsgroups provide valuable methods of 'meeting' potential employers, employees, collaborators and customers. If you filter your newsgroup list with the word **job** you'll see a number of useful groups, including **alt.jobs**, **alt.jobs.overseas**, and an entire **uk.jobs** hierarchy that includes **uk.jobs.offered** and **uk.jobs.wanted**. It's well worth looking for newsgroups catering for your particular profession or vocation too: sometimes the only way to learn of a job opportunity is to be on 'speaking terms' with the type of people who can point you in the right direction.

Pursue your Hobbies & Interests

In This Chapter...

➪ Read online versions of leisure and specialist magazines

➪ Find other Internet users who share your hobbies

➪ Where to seek advice and support on the Net

➪ Follow your favourite sports, teams and players online

➪ See the sights of the world without leaving home

However solitary a pursuit your hobby is, it probably isn't something you like to follow completely alone. Whether you like gardening, fishing, stamp collecting, or origami, part of the enjoyment is in being able to talk about it with other enthusiasts, share knowledge and skills and just chat.

The Internet can, of course, help in this department, but far from just being a place to air your origami anecdotes, it can teach you more about your hobby, give you advice and support on a range of issues, and help you to organise your own clubs and societies.

Read your favourite magazines online

The chances are good (and getting better all the time) that your favourite magazine has an online edition in the form of a Web site. If so, the URL will probably be listed somewhere in the magazine itself, but it's worth visiting a search engine and typing its name into a keyword search. If that doesn't work, it's a racing certainty that there's an online magazine somewhere that fits the bill, so try a search in the form magazine *your hobby*.

To point you in the right direction, two of the UK's biggest magazine publishers have sites containing all their magazines in online form. Head along to mag.net (home of VNU Publications) at **http://www.vnu.co.uk**,

---

 NET TIP

Pros & cons of online magazines

Online versions of magazines are usually free, but you pay a price of sorts. Often the online version will be 'published' a week or two later than the paper version, and it may not be a complete copy. In their favour, though, you can save a small fortune if you normally buy several magazines every month, and you can store interesting articles on disk rather than snipping out pages!

---

or FutureNet (Future Publishing's site) at
http://www.futurenet.co.uk, and fill in the registration
forms to get free access to dozens of major magazines.
But, in case that's not enough, here's a few more:

Magazine	Web site URL
Cosmopolitan	http://www.designercity.com/cosmopolitan
Esquire	http://www.designercity.com/esquire/index.htm
Exchange and Mart	http://www.exchangeandmart.co.uk
Horse and Rider	http://www.equestrian.co.uk
Loaded	http://www.uploaded.com
Q magazine	http://www.erack.com/qweb
Reader's Digest	http://www.readersdigest.co.uk
Select	http://www.erack.com/select
Top Gear magazine	http://www.topgear.com

Still haven't found the magazine you're looking for?
Yahoo! lists a full 20 categories of magazine at
**http://www.yahoo.co.uk/Regional/Countries/United_
Kingdom/News_and_Media/Magazines**.

Get in touch with other enthusiasts

The most obvious way to make contact with others
who share your hobby is through Usenet. The **rec.** and
talk. hierarchies cover an amazingly vast number of
interests between them, but if you find that
yours isn't there, use your newsreader's filter option
to find it – surely if a group like **alt.macdonalds.
ketchup** can exist, there must be something there
for you!

Share it on the Web

The majority of Web sites are created by personal users like you and me who want to share their interests, so why not join them? As well as being a satisfying achievement, it adds another opportunity for meeting people (as long as you include your email address).

There are bound to be sites on the World Wide Web relating to your hobby, and a keyword search in your favourite search engine should find them. It's a safe bet that anyone creating a Web site on a particular topic is an enthusiast, so why not check the site for an email address and get in touch?

Support & advice at your fingertips

The Internet is the ideal place to find advice and support groups for any issue imaginable. In some cases, the Net is the only way you could ever access these services – if they exist in the 'real world' at all, they may be based on a different continent! If you know the name of an established organisation or group, you might be able to find it on the Web using a search engine. Otherwise, use a descriptive keyword search such as **advice legal** or **support disability**. Here's a brief taste of some of the help available – you'll find links to more sites on the accompanying CD-ROM.

▷ Law Lounge is a complete one-stop free legal advice centre that can also point you to UK solicitors and barristers, law schools, and a range of other services. Visit **http://www.lawlounge.com**.

▷ For consumer advice, go to **http://www.oft.gov.uk** at the Office of Fair Trading. The site is split into categories including Credit & Debt, Holiday Problems, How To Complain, and General Consumer Rights.

⇨ If you're looking for some straightforward health tips, why not head off to CyberDiet at **http://www.cyberdiet.com**. Despite its name, the site covers all aspects of healthy living and provides copious tips.

Passively reading a Web page may give you the information you need, but in some cases you'll want to draw on the experiences of others. In one recent case, after being told that nothing could be done for her child, a mother appealed for help in a support newsgroup and learned of a potentially life-saving operation in South America. There are many such newsgroups available – either filter your list with the word **support**, or take a look at the extensive **alt.support** hierarchy.

Share your interests with a penpal

This is really one for the kids – after all, grown-ups have Usenet largely to themselves, don't they? There's quite a range of sites that can put you in touch with an email penpal, and you can find a good selection of them at **http://www.yahoo.co.uk/ Society_and_Culture/Friendship/Pen_Pals/Kids**. The best, though, is KeyPals at

How do my kids know that their penpals really are kids?

They don't, necessarily, so a little parental involvement would be wise in the early stages. However, if an adult was up to no good, he'd be more likely to initiate contact himself than to register at KeyPals and wait for kids to contact him. A little extra caution is advisable when your kids receive unsolicited email.

http://www.kidpub.org/kidpub/keypals, shown in the next screenshot. As with most penpal search sites, you can enter an age (from 6 to 16) and location for your perfect penpal, but the bonus at KeyPals is that you can specify an interest too.

The search results appear as a list of people's names, locations and ages. These are all hypertext mail links, so clicking one of these should start your email program and open a blank message window with the penpal's email address already inserted.

keypal-search.html at www.kidpub.org - Microsoft Internet Explorer

File   Edit   View   Go   Favorites   Help

KidPub

KeyPals

KidPub KeyPals Search Form

Select the kind of KeyPal you want to write to, then hit the SEARCH button. You can leave the 'interested in' box empty if you like.

Ok, for a KeyPal I'm looking for a

| boy or girl ▾ | around age | any ▾ | who lives in | Anywhere / Alabama / Alaska |

and is interested in [   ]

Start Searching!

Find penpals from all over the world at KeyPals

For a wider choice of penpals, and some casual online chat into the bargain, take a look at the newsgroups. By far the most popular is **soc.penpals**, but you'll also find plenty of movement going on in **alt.kids-talk.penpals** and **alt.teens.penpals**.

Keep up with your favourite sport

Whatever your sport, you'll find it on the Net in abundance – team Web sites, sporting facts and figures, fan pages, fantasy games, and much more. The search engines are your key to finding these sites, as usual, by entering the name of your sport, team, or player, but here are a few links to get you started:

Sports site	Web address
Adidas Webzine	http://www.adidas.com
Athletics World Records	http://www.hkkk.fi/ ~ niininen/athl.html
Formula 1	http://www.f1-live..com/GB
GolfWeb Europe	http://www.golfweb.com/europe
Ladbrokes... Super Sports Service	http://www.sports.ladbrokes.co.uk
Paralympic Games	http://info.lut.ac.uk/research/paad/ipc/ipc.html
Rugby Leaguer	http://www.rugbyleaguer.co.uk
Tennis	http://www.tennis.com

If you're a football fan, don't waste your time tracking down a team-page with the search engines. Head straight for the Soccer City site at **http://athene.net/soccercity** instead. Here you'll find links to over 3000 (count the zeros!) Web pages of UK soccer clubs, covering both official team sites and fan pages.

For almost any sports fan, the *Sporting Life's* online

The Sporting Life site should be a regular port of call for all sports fans

edition (**http://www.sporting-life.com**) is a good candidate for your Favorites menu, covering Soccer, Rugby, Racing, Golf, Cricket, and more, together with the latest sports news and a messages centre. You'll also find some of the most popular sporting magazines at Future Publishing's site, mentioned earlier in this chapter.

Track down your favourite celebrity

Everyone wants to know what their favourite film star, band or singer is up to, and you'll find at least one Web site devoted to every celebrity you've ever heard of (and quite a few that you haven't). Visits to some of these sites can turn up biographies, interviews, photos, movie clips, and the latest reviews and news. You can use a search engine to track down these pages by entering the celebrity's name, but it's helpful to know how your chosen engine works before you do so. If it allows you to, enclose the name in quote signs (such as **"Jennifer Aniston"**) so that you'll only see pages in which both names appear. Alternatively, prefix each name with a plus sign (**+Jennifer +Aniston**).

If all that seems a little complicated, start by visiting Yahoo! You'll find a massive list of links to movie-star pages at **http://www.yahoo.co.uk/ Entertainment/Movies_and_Films/Actors_and_ Actresses**. The list of musical artists is longer still, and has had to be split alphabetically: head off to **http://www.yahoo.co.uk/Entertainment/Music/Artists** and click an initial letter at the top of the page

---

The sounds of the stars

If you're looking for interviews with the stars, visit BiteSite at **http://www.bitesite.com**. This site features hundreds of interviews and plays them using streaming RealAudio sound (see Chapter 15), although you can read text transcripts if you prefer.

corresponding to the name of the band or the surname of the artist you're looking for. Most fan pages contain links to other fan pages, so when you've found your way to one you'll probably have easy access to the best sites around.

For news and chat, celebrities have a similar level of coverage in the newsgroups as they do on the Web. There are large **alt.fan** and **alt.music** hierarchies with groups dedicated to specific artists such as **alt.music.paul-simon** and **alt.fan.james-bond**, plus more general groups like **alt.music.midi** and **alt.music.bluegrass**.

Take a cyber-sightseeing tour

One interest that most of us share is an ambition to 'see the world' – that vague term that encompasses natural and architectural wonders, famous works of art, and the ruins of ancient kingdoms. The trouble is, unless you're extremely wealthy and have no pressing

Sight	Web address
Golden Gate Bridge	http://www.mcn.org/goldengate/index.html
Grand Canyon	http://www.kaibab.org
Great Barrier Reef	http://werple.mira.net.au/~margaret/frames1.htm
Leaning Tower of Pisa	http://www.cibernet.it/thebox/pisa/tower.html
Le Louvre	http://mistral.culture.fr/louvre/louvrea.htm
Mount Rushmore	http://www.state.sd.us/tourism/rushmore/rushmore.html
Seven Wonders of the Ancient World	http://pharos.bu.edu/Egypt/Wonders/
Yellowstone National Park	http://www.yellowstone-natl-park.com

engagements for the next few years, it's a difficult ambition to realise.

Fortunately, the sights that we'd happily travel for days to see are just a few clicks away on the Internet, and can usually be found with a keyword search. Many of these Web sites include background information too, but if you need a little more depth you might be able to find a 'travelogue' site created by someone who's actually visited that country – try a search for **travelogue** *country*. To save you a little searching time, a few of the sights you're probably itching to see are listed on the previous page.

Sightseeing closer to home

Of course, the United Kingdom can boast its own places of interest, and you don't have to travel for days to see them. Many now have Web sites that can tell you how to get there, when to visit, and what you'll have to pay to get in. Better still, you'll find enough information on some of these sites that you don't even have to set foot outside!

A good example is the HMS Belfast, which you'll find on the River Thames at Tower Bridge, and on the Web at **http://www.hmsbelfast.org.uk**. Along with

One of many online exhibitions at the London Science Museum

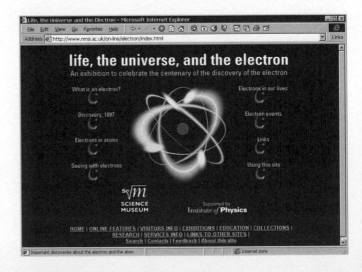

fascinating historical information, you can take a full photographic guided tour, find out what fo'c'sle, messdeck and grog are all about, and link to live-camera views of the Belfast and other sites of the Thames.

When you've finished kicking around the quarterdeck, how about a look at the Imperial War Museum (**http://www.iwm.org.uk**) which also incorporates Whitehall's Cabinet War Rooms and the Duxford Airfield. In fact, if you're a keen museum-goer, you'll find plenty to keep you busy on the Web. The National Museum of Science and Industry at **http://www.nmsi.ac.uk** includes the London Science Museum, The National Railway Museum at York, and Bradford's Museum of Photography, Film & Television. Want to try a few more?

Museum	Web address
Beaulieu National Motor Museum	http://www.itl.net/features/nmm
British Museum	http://www.british-museum.ac.uk
Dickens House Museum	http://www.rmplc.co.uk/orgs/dickens
Natural History Museum	http://www.nhm.ac.uk
Victoria & Albert Museum	http://www.vam.ac.uk

So much for the great indoors. Perhaps you're more interested in the natural world. If so, an ideal starting point is Naturenet at **http://www.naturenet.net**. This site gathers links to all manner of UK nature-related sites from environmental and political issues to county-by-county listings of country parks and nature reserves (many of which have web sites of their own) and organisations such as The National Trust, The Woodland Trust, Plantlife and The Countryside Commission.

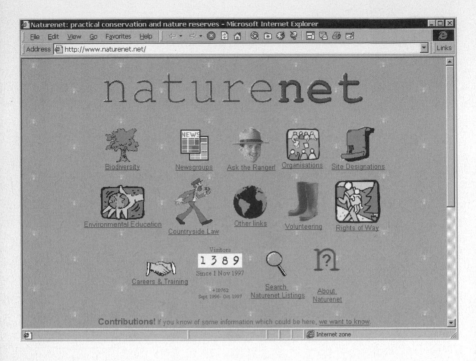

Naturenet's
comprehensive
links make this
the ideal starting
point for nature
lovers

Weird Science – Web Multimedia

In This Chapter...

▷ Getting the best out of the Web's multimedia elements

▷ Listen to music & live radio with RealAudio

▷ View and download clips of favourite movies

▷ Virtual Reality – fly through 3-dimensional online worlds

▷ Live camera feeds and remote robot control via the Web

By now, you should have a good idea of how much you can accomplish using your Internet connection. Without a doubt, the sheer scope of its content, together with its convenience, helps to explain the Net's popularity.

But that's not all of it. The main reason for this popularity surge is that it's now fun to use – today's World Wide Web launches an all-out assault on your senses with animation, sound and video to give you a true multimedia experience.

In this chapter, you'll learn about the different multimedia elements used on the Web and some of the advanced technologies that ordinary users invest their time and money in purely for our benefit. But first, a more pressing question...

Do you need a better computer for multimedia?

Multimedia is a sort of ex-buzzword. In 1996, a 'multimedia computer' had all the trimmings and cost a lot more than its non-multimedia counterpart. Today, however, the word is rarely attached to computers – almost all new computers have a soundcard, CD-ROM drive, and a capable graphics card, which are the essentials of multimedia. But here's a quick hardware rundown for *good* multimedia:

▷ If your graphics card has 2Mb or more of memory fitted, letting you display more than 256 colours, visual elements like videos and virtual reality worlds will be clearer, smoother, and generally more appealing.

▷ Some of the larger virtual worlds take their toll on both processor and memory: ideally, you should have at least a Pentium 120MHz processor and a minimum 16Mb RAM.

▷ The modem matters most. If you connect at less than 28.8Kbps, you'll just find the whole experience frustratingly slow. Movies and virtual worlds, in particular, can be huge files, so buy the fastest modem your service provider supports if these appeal to you.

Do you need a lot of extra software?

There are literally hundreds of plug-ins and viewers out there for different types of multimedia file, and you certainly don't want them all! Some, of course, cover the same types of file as others and you can simply choose the one you like best. Others are proprietary programs that let you view a type of file created by one particular company – if this format isn't in wide use on the Web you might prefer not to bother installing the software for it.

What's the difference between a plug-in and a viewer?

A plug-in is a program that displays a file in your browser's own window by adding capabilities to your browser that it doesn't have already. A viewer is an entirely separate program that opens its own window to display or play a file you've downloaded.

Here are two suggestions to simplify things. First, start with the software mentioned in this chapter and in the 'Top 5' list at the end of Chapter 9. Second, buy an uninstall utility such as Quarterdeck's CleanSweep. these utilities monitor every change and addition made to your system when a new program is installed so that you can remove all trace of it later if you decide you don't like it.

RealAudio – the sound of cyberspace

You won't travel far on the Web before arriving at a site that uses RealAudio for music, speech, or a mixture of the two. RealAudio is a streaming format that plays as the file is being transferred, with none of that tedious waiting around for the sound file to download first. As soon as you click a RealAudio link, your RealAudio Player opens (as in the next screenshot), grabs the first few seconds of the transmission to help it to stay one jump ahead and ensure smooth playback, and then starts to play. You can pause or stop playback by clicking the appropriate buttons, or replay the entire clip from the beginning. If you have Internet Explorer you don't need to do anything more – the RealAudio plug-in is bundled with it. If you're using a different browser, you'll have to visit **http://www.realaudio.com** to download and install the player software.

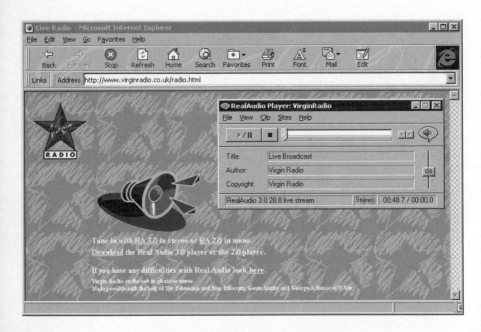

A live RealAudio broadcast from Virgin Radio

So, where do you have to go to get some RealAudio action? As with all multimedia plug-ins and viewers, your first stop should be the Web site of the people who wrote the program – you'll always find plenty of samples and links to let you play with your new toy once you've installed it. In this case, then, skip off to **http://www.realaudio.com**.

▷ Why not tune in to Virgin Radio which can be found at **http://www.virginradio.co.uk** to hear the wireless come down the wires?

▷ Want to hear the Top 40? Visit London's Capital Radio at **http://www.capital-fm.co.uk**, click the **Top 40** link and click the **RealAudio** icon beside the chart hit you'd like to hear – you can even buy your CD singles here! Or click **On Air** to hear the live broadcast.

▷ Check out BiteSite at **http://www.bitesite.com** for RealAudio interviews with the stars.

Other sound formats

RealAudio doesn't offer great sound quality – some sacrifices have to be made for the files to transfer this fast. Top-quality sound comes in the form of **.wav** files, which Internet Explorer can play without any extra help, and these weigh in at up to 10 megabytes for a top-quality one-minute file! Smaller .mid files require a MIDI-capable (preferably wavetable) soundcard. Both .wav and .mid files have to be downloaded in their entirety before they can be played.

It's movie time... soon!

First things first. Video files are big! A one-minute movie will be roughly 2.5 megabytes, and in most cases you'll have to wait for the whole thing to download before you can watch it. With a 28.8Kbps modem, you're looking at ten to fifteen minutes' boredom for your one minute of entertainment. All the same, as with most multimedia elements, it pays to have the software installed just in case you come across something that really seems worth the wait!

The three most common types of movie file on the Web are MPEG (which will have **.mpeg**, **.mpg** or **.mpe** extensions), QuickTime (**.mov** or **.qt**), and Video For Windows (**.avi**). If you've installed Internet Explorer, you should already have a program called ActiveMovie which can play each of these types. ActiveMovie works as both a browser plug-in and a separate viewer that you can use to playback movies offline.

Although ActiveMovie is a useful program, it doesn't always handle MPEG videos correctly, and isn't completely compatible with QuickTime. Here are two other programs well worth adding to your collection:

▷ **QuickTime Player**. There are various types of QuickTime file, including audio and Virtual Reality, and this program was built to handle them all. Grab it from **http://www.quicktime.apple.com**.

▷ **Net Toob**. An all-purpose plug-in and viewer that handles just about every video and audio file you'll come across. It can also stream some types of MPEG movie to prevent that agonising wait. You can download the shareware Net Toob from **http://www.nettoob.com**.

Ready to watch some videos? For over 1300 QuickTime clips from cinema films, head for the QuickTime Archive at **http://film.softcenter.se/flics** and browse the alphabetical list for the name of the film you want. One of the best starting points for MPEG movies is the MPEG Monster List at **http://www.islandnet.com/ ~ carleton/monster/**

Saturday Night at the Movies. (But I started downloading on Tuesday!)

monster.html, which lists MPEG resources and information, links to more plug-ins, and a truly monster list of movie sites on the Web. Or try Bryan's cute animations at **http://www.oas.omron.com/bryan/anims.html**. Finally, don't forget to visit the QuickTime Web site mentioned above – you'll find a Samples page with links to some superb sites.

The hot topic — cool animation

The word animation doesn't sound cool – it probably reminds you of Bugs Bunny – but it's a major multimedia craze on the Internet. Where images and text have always been fixed on the page, they can now move around and react to the mouse passing over them. Part of this popularity lies in the fact that animations are easier for the average user to create than videos, and they take no more time to download than an image.

It gets better! The two hottest types of animation are Macromedia's ShockWave and Flash, both of which you can view in Internet Explorer without adding anything else to your software mountain. If you're not using Explorer, though, you'll have to head off to **http://www.macromedia.com** to download the necessary plug-ins.

 How can I add these animations to my own Web pages?

Flash animations are reasonably simple to create using Macromedia's Flash software, which includes excellent interactive tutorials. You can download a trial version which you'll find at **http://www.macromedia.com**, but be prepared to spend some serious money if you decide to continue using it!

The list of animation sites is almost endless – you'll keep seeing them on the Web, unless you're actually looking for one: that's how the world works, isn't it? So here are a few to let you see what all the fuss is about:

▷ Visit Macromedia's Flash Gallery at **http://www.macromedia.com/shockzone/edge/flash** for links to some of the Flash-iest sites on the Web.

▷ Try the Cool ShockWave Site Of The Week at **http://www.shocker.com/shocker/cool.html**.

▷ You'll find a nice ShockWave site, with links to more, if you head off to The Shockade at **http://www.expanse.com/shockade/index.htm**.

▷ For a bit of overkill in the Flash department, visit the Microsoft Network at **http://www.msn.com**.

The MSN homepage — if it holds still, click it!

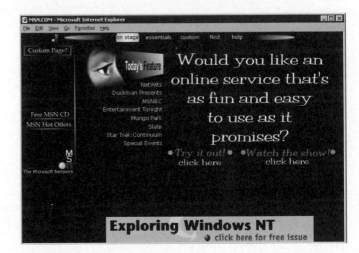

Explore virtual 3D worlds

Virtual Reality is something that's either going to grab you immediately and not let go, or leave you wondering why anyone would bother. Using on-screen controls (often combined with right mouse-button menus), you can select angles from which to view the scene, walk or fly through it, zoom in and out, and in the more recent VRML 2.0 format, interact with objects you find. True VRML files have the extension **.wrl** (although they're often accompanied by a collection of GIF images that form various elements of the world), and you'll need to install a plug-in before you can start exploring.

VRML

An abbreviation of Virtual Reality Modelling Language, the programming language used to build these graphical 'worlds'. The original version of the language was 1.0; the latest version, 2.0, adds new features such as the ability to pick up and move virtual objects.

In fact, there are many companies also producing proprietary plug-ins for their own brands of 3D world, but it's best to pause awhile and see if Virtual Reality is your cup of tea. Most VRML plug-ins are large programs, and the worlds themselves can be slow to download and slow-moving once you start to explore – you'll definitely benefit from a fast Internet connection and a fast processor! That being said, VRML is a whole new experience you've got to try at least once, so grab one of these .wrl plug-ins:

▷ **Superscape Viscape** from **http://www.superscape.com** You'll find a world full of more virtual worlds hosted by Superscape at **http://vwww.com**.

▷ **WIRL** from **http://www.platinum.com.** A large plug-in which adds a few extra facilities to ordinary VRML. These come into their own when you start exploring the unusually fast and interactive worlds you'll find at the same site.

If you've followed the links from these sites and you still need more, why not visit Planet 9 at **http://www.planet9.com** to cruise through virtual American cities, or **http://nowtv.com/vrml/index.htm** to play 3-dimensional online games with other visitors to the site. If you fancy something that loads a little quicker, Protozoa's weird 3D interactive creatures at **http://protozoa.protozoa.com/vrml_scenes** fit the bill nicely, downloading in not much more than 30 seconds.

Where can I find other plug-ins?

You'll find the best selection at Tucows, it's a great site for Internet-related software. Head for **http://tucows.cableinet.net/window95.html** and click the **Browser Plug-ins** heading. While you're there, take a look at **ActiveX Plug-ins** for Internet Explorer.

Catch the action with live cam

Here's an unusual branch of cyberspace. People who probably seem outwardly quite sane spend their hard-earned money on a special type of camera, rig it up to the Web via some complicated programming and a (usually) permanent Internet connection, and then point it at a street corner, or their desk, or a fish-bowl... almost anything that moves, in fact.

The oddest thing about live cam sites is that many of them really are entertaining! As an example, point your browser at the corner of Hollywood and Vine (**http://hollywood.bhi.hollywood.ca.us:8000/pictures/image01.gif**), and refresh the image every few seconds. You'll see the traffic lights changing, vehicles passing, people walking in and out of shot... and the longer you have to wait for something to actually move, the more rewarding it is when it happens. There are thousands of Web cameras running all over the

Push or pull?

We met 'push technology' in Chapter 12, where it was being used to send news stories down the wires to your computer. Some live-cam sites use the same system to send an updated camera view every few seconds or minutes. At many sites, though, you'll have to 'pull' – in other words, to view a newer picture, click Internet Explorer's Refresh button, or press F5.

world, some providing pure zany entertainment, others giving more practical information (such as up-to-the-minute pictures of your chosen holiday destination). Here's a taste of a few more.

▷ Visit **http://www.netlinkservices.com/cam.htm** to see if Lee is working at his computers.

▷ See the Manhattan skyline from the top of the Empire State Building by visiting **http://www.realtech.com/webcam**.

▷ Take a look inside Jason's office by going to **http://george.lbl.gov/cgi-bin/jason/cave-cam**.

▷ Find out what Cujo the parrot is doing today (although he's not what you'd call a busy parrot), at **http://www.spies.com/arubin**.

▷ Find a huge collection of links to more informative or entertaining web-cams on Tommy's List at **http://www.rt66.com/ ~ ozone/cam.htm**.

The mesmerising TurtleCam at **http://www.campusware.com/turtles**

This page will Refresh itself every 60 seconds!

Robots in cyberspace

If you prefer a little more interactivity, you can find robots hooked up to the World Wide Web too. Some have cameras trained on them so that you can see what they're doing; others are actually mobile, with cameras attached to act as 'eyes'. The level of technology involved and the logistics of making it work are staggering, so there are relatively few robot sites on the Web, and you might have to wait some time before you can take a turn at controlling a robot yourself. At most sites you'll be assigned control for only a few minutes – make sure you read the instructions while you're waiting so that you'll know how the controls work when your turn comes around.

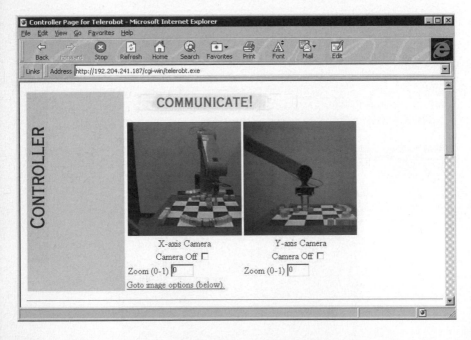

Tell Telerobot where to put its building blocks

A good place to start is Telerobot at **http://192.204.241.187/cgi-win/telerobt.exe**, where your task is to arrange building blocks into satisfying shapes. Not only are the controls easy to understand, but the images are unusually clear and in colour. Another enjoyable robot worth trying is Xavier (**http://www.cs.cmu.edu/People/Xavier**), who roams through an office building according to your commands. Xavier's a popular chap, though, and he keeps US business hours, so he can be a little hard to reach.

For a more calming use of cyber-robotics, visit the Telegarden at **http://telegarden.aec.at/index.html**. By clicking **Guest Entrance** (followed by **Enter Garden** on the next page), you can watch this horticultural robot at work. Alternatively, if you register as a member, you can water the garden and plant seeds by remote control, and leave messages online for other members.

uilding your own Web Site

In This Chapter...

⇨ A simple Web page: title, heading and paragraphs

⇨ Formatting text with bold and italic type

⇨ Inserting links to other pages and Web sites

⇨ Spicing up the page with colour and images

I n the previous chapters you've learnt how to use just about every area of the Internet – the major services, the search engines, multimedia, the whole shebang – but it's still everyone else's Internet you're using!

Sooner or later you'll want to grab a little corner of it and make it your own. The mechanics of creating a Web site are simple enough, and in this chapter you'll learn how to do it. Of course, whole books have been written on this subject so this isn't an exhaustive reference, but it should get you off to a flying start. There are many guides and tutorials on the Web itself which can help you improve your skills, and you'll find two of the best at:

http://www.asiweb.com/htmlauth.htm.
http://www.ncsa.uiuc.edu/General/Internet/WWW
/HTMLPrimer.html.

HTML – the language of the Web

Pages on the World Wide Web are written in a language called **HTML** (HyperText Markup Language). So what's that all about? Well, we've met hypertext already – those underlined, clickable links that make the Web so easy to navigate. A markup language is a set of codes or signs added to plain text to indicate how it should be presented to the reader, noting bold or italic text, typefaces to be used, paragraph breaks, and so on. When you type any document into your word-processor, it adds these codes for you, but tactfully hides them from view: if you wanted bold text, for example, it shows you bold text instead of those codes. In HTML, however, you have to type in the codes yourself along with the text, and your browser puts the whole lot together before displaying it.

These codes are known as **tags**, and they consist of ordinary text placed between less-than and greater-than signs. Let's take an example:

< B > Welcome to my homepage. < /B > Glad you could make it!

The first tag, < B >, means 'turn on bold type'. Halfway through the line, the same tag is used again, but with a forward slash inserted straight after the less-than sign: this means 'turn off bold type'. If you displayed a page containing this line in your browser, it would look like this:

Welcome to my homepage. Glad you could make it!

Of course, there's more to a Web page than bold text, so clearly there must be many more of these tags. But don't let that worry you – you don't have to learn all of them! There's a small bundle that you'll use a lot, and you'll get to know those very quickly. The rest will begin to sink in once you've used them a few times.

Do you need special software?

Believe it or not, creating a Web site is something you can do for free (once you've bought a computer and started paying for an Internet connection, that is). Because HTML is entirely text-based, you can write your pages in Windows' Notepad, and we'll assume that's what you're doing. But there are other options, so let's quickly run through them.

WYSIWYG

A delightful acronym (pronounced 'wizzywig') for 'What you see is what you get'. This is used to describe many different types of software that can show you on the screen exactly what something will look like when you print it on paper or view it in your Web browser.

WYSIWYG editors

In theory, WYSIWYG editors are the perfect way of working: instead of looking at plain text with HTML tags dotted around it, you see your Web page itself gradually taking shape, with images, colours and formatting displayed. There are a couple of drawbacks. First, WYSIWYG editors cost serious money compared to most other types of Internet software. Second, they probably won't help you avoid learning something about HTML. Once in a while the editor won't do what you want it to do, and you'll have to switch to its text-editing mode to juggle the tags yourself. You may find that it's far easier to learn the language itself than it is to learn how the WYSIWYG software works, but if you'd like to give the WYSIWYG method a shot, here are two of the most popular programs:

▷ **Microsoft FrontPage.** You can find out more about this at **http://www.microsoft.com/frontpage**, but you'll have to take a trip into town to buy a copy. (Windows 98 users already have a cut-down version of FrontPage called FrontPage Express.)

▷ **Adobe PageMill.** Visit **http://www.adobe.com/ prodindex/pagemill/main.html** for details, downloads and online payment.

Markup editors
Using a markup editor is rather like using Notepad – you see all the HTML codes on the page in front of you. But instead of having to type in tags yourself, a

Colour-coding and one-click tag insertion in HomeSite

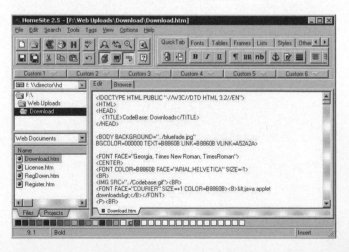

markup editor will insert them for you at the click of a button or the press of a hotkey, in the same way that you use your word-processor. You might still choose to type in some of the simple tags yourself, such as the tag for bold text mentioned earlier, but for more complicated elements such as a table with a lot of cells, this automation is a great time and sanity saver.

Markup editors are also ideal for newcomers to HTML. If you don't know one tag from another, just click the appropriate buttons on the toolbar to insert them: once you've seen them appear on the page a few times, you'll soon start to remember what's what!

Here are three of the most popular and feature-packed markup editors. You'll need to register these if you want to use them beyond the trial period.

▷ **HomeSite** from **http://www.dexnet.com/homesite**.

▷ **WebEdit PRO** from **http://www.luckman.com**.

▷ **HTMLed** from **http://www.ist.ca**.

Text converters

Some modern word-processors like Lotus WordPro and Microsoft Word have begun to include features to turn your documents into Web pages. At their simplest, they'll let you create an ordinary word-processed document and then choose a **Save as HTML** option from the File menu to convert it into a Web page. The

Using Office on the Web

If you use Microsoft Office 97, the Web authoring features don't stop at Word. Excel allows you to save a worksheet in HTML format, and PowerPoint helps you create multimedia pages by converting slides to Web format. You'll also find a media library of pictures, sounds and animations that you can include in your pages, however you choose to create them.

result won't be as effective as other pages on the Web, but it's an ideal way to convert a long document when the only other option is to add all the tags yourself!

You can also create Web pages from scratch in these programs. For example, Microsoft Word has its own Web Page Wizard that can set you up with a ready-to-edit template. To start it up, go to **File | New...**, then click the **Web Pages** tab and double-click **Web Page Wizard**. You can add and delete elements on the page, and use the standard drawing and editing toolbars to slot in anything else you need.

Let's get started

There are a few bits and pieces that will appear in almost every HTML document you write, so let's start by making a template file you can use every time you want to create a new page. Start Notepad, and type the text below (without worrying about the exact number of spaces or carriage returns). Save this file using any name you like, but make sure you give it the extension **.htm** or **.html**. Every Web page you write must be saved with one of these extensions – it doesn't matter which you choose, but you'll find life a lot easier if you stick to the same one each time!

```
< !DOCTYPE HTML PUBLIC "-//W3C//DTD
   HTML 3.2//EN" >

< HTML >
< HEAD >
   < TITLE > Untitled < /TITLE >
< /HEAD >

< BODY >

< /BODY >
< /HTML >
```

None of those tags does anything exciting by itself, but it's worth knowing what they're all for. The first line is a piece of technical nonsense that tells a browser that the document is written in the latest version of the HTML language. The rest of the document is placed between the < HTML > and </HTML > tags, and falls into two separate chunks: the **head** (the section between < HEAD > and </HEAD >) and the **body** (between < BODY > and </BODY >)

The document's head is pretty dull: all it contains is the title of the document, inserted between the < TITLE > and </TITLE > tags. There are other bits and pieces that can be slotted in here, but the title is the only element that must be included.

Do I have to type these tags in capitals?

No. Browsers don't care about the case of the tags. If you prefer < title >, or < Title >, or even < tItLe >, it's all the same to your browser. But typing tags in capitals makes them stand out from the rest of your text, which can be useful for editing.

The body section is the one that matters. Between these two tags you'll type the text that should appear on your page, and put in the tags you need to display images, set colours, insert hyperlinks to other pages and sites, and anything else you want your page to contain.

Now that you've created a basic template, let's start adding to it to build up a respectable-looking page.

Add a title and text

The first thing to do is to replace the word **Untitled** with a sensible title for the document, such as **Links To The Best Multimedia Sites** or **My EastEnders HomePage**. Pick something that describes what the page will be about, but keep it fairly short: the text between the < TITLE > and </TITLE > tags will appear in the title-bar at the very top of most browsers, and if your entry is too long to fit it will just get chopped off!

Now we'll add some text to the page. Either type the same text as in the example below, or replace the first and second paragraph entries with whole paragraphs if you prefer. When you've done that, save the file as **links.html**, but don't close your Notepad just yet.

```
< !DOCTYPE HTML PUBLIC "-//W3C//DTD HTML
   3.2//EN" >

< HTML >
< HEAD >
   < TITLE > Links To The Best Multimedia Sites < /TITLE >
< /HEAD >

< BODY >
< H1 > Welcome To My Homepage! < /H1 >
Here's the first paragraph.
< P > And here's the second paragraph.

< /BODY >
< /HTML >
```

Now take a look at your masterpiece in your browser. There are several ways you can do this: find the file you just saved and double-click it, or open your browser and type the path to the file in the address bar, or choose **File | Open** and click on **Browse**. When your browser displays it, it should look just like the next screenshot.

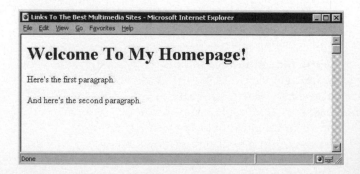

So what are those new tags all about? Let's take the < P > tag first. This tells your browser to present the following text as a new paragraph, automatically inserting a blank line before it. And this raises an important point about HTML: you can't insert blank lines just by pressing Enter or Return. Although you can see blank lines in Notepad when you do that, your browser will just ignore them, which is why you need to start a new paragraph by entering < P >. (Notice that you don't have to put in a closing < /P > at the end of a paragraph – the act of starting a new paragraph isn't an ongoing effect that has to be turned off again.)

How do I start a new line without starting a new paragraph?

Another tag, < BR >, will give you a 'line break'. In other words, the text that follows that tag will start at the beginning of the next line with no empty line inserted before it.

The other pair of tags that cropped up was < H1 > and < /H1 > which format a line of text as a heading. You can choose from six sizes: < H1 > is the largest, followed by < H2 > and < /H2 > down to the smallest, < H6 > and < /H6 >. In one nifty little manoeuvre, these tags change the size of the text you place between them and make it bold. They also auto-matically start a new paragraph for the heading (so you don't need to place a < P > tag at the start of the line), and start a new paragraph for whatever follows the heading. Try changing the size of the heading by altering those tags to see the different effects, re-saving the file, and clicking your browser's Refresh button to update it.

Be bold. (Or be italic...)

The tags for bold and italic text are easy to remember: < B > for bold, and < I > for italic. As both of these

are ongoing effects, you'll have to enter closing tags
(</B> or </I>) when you want the effect to stop.
And, just as in your word-processor, you can combine
these tags, so if your document contained this:

This is <I>italic</I>. This is <B>bold</B>.
This is <B><I>bold & italic</I></B>.

the result would look like this in your browser:

This is *italic*. This is **bold**. This is ***bold & italic***.

Lesser-used text-formatting tags that might come in
handy one day are superscript (^{and})
and subscript (_{and}). If you really
feel the urge, you can underline text using another
memorable pair of tags, <U> and </U>, but be
careful how you use underlining: web-surfers expect
underlined text to be a hyperlink, and might find your
gratuitous use of these tags confusing.

Spaces in HTML

NET TIP

Just as browsers ignore your use of the Enter or Return key when
you create your Web pages, they have a similar attitude to the
Spacebar. However many spaces you enter in a row, only the first
will be recognised. If you really need more than one space, type in
the code   for each space you want (so by entering
    you would insert three spaces).

Insert links to other sites

It's an unwritten rule that a Web site should contain
links to other Web sites. After all, the entire Web works
by being inter-connected, and if people surf their way
to your site and have to retrace their steps before they
can continue surfing, they'll steer clear in future! So
let's put in another <P> tag to start a new paragraph,
and add that sorely-needed link as shown below:

< P > Visit Macromedia's snazzy < A HREF =
"http://www.macromedia.com/shockzone" >
Shockzone < /A > site.

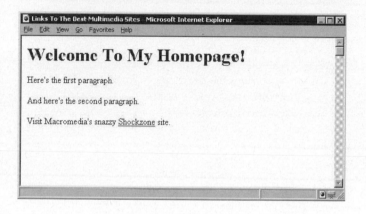

This is a more complicated tag, so let's look at it bit
by bit. Although we call these 'links', in HTML they're
called **anchors**, and that's where the A comes from
after the first < sign. An anchor usually begins with
the < A HREF = tag. Following that comes the URL of
the page you want to link to, always enclosed in
double-quotes, and the > sign to finish the opening
anchor tag.

Immediately after the opening anchor tag, type the
text you want visitors to your page to click on. This
might be a single word, a sentence, or even a whole
paragraph, but don't forget to put something here, or
there'll be nothing to click on to reach that site! Finally,
type the closing anchor tag, < /A > .

Get it central

NET TIP

You can place elements centrally on the page by placing them
between < CENTER > and < /CENTER > tags (note the American
spelling, though!). This applies to headings, paragraphs of text,
images, and almost anything else you might want to include.

Links to other pages on your own site

The link we just added used something called an **absolute URL**. In fact, that's the only type of URL you've seen so far: an absolute URL gives the whole path to the page you want to open, including the http:// prefix and the name of the computer. When you want to create links to other pages on your own site you can use a different, simpler method.

Create a new HTML document, and save it to the directory where the other is stored. Let's assume you've called it **morelinks.html**. Now, in your first document, you can create a link to this new page by typing this anchor:

> < A HREF = "morelinks.html" > Here's a few more links. < /A >

Yes, it's just a filename. This is called a **relative URL**. It tells your browser to look for a file called **morelinks.html** and display it. The great thing about relative URLs is that you can test these on your own system to make sure they work: for absolute URLs, your PC would have to connect to your IAP to search for the page. Since the browser hasn't been told where else to look, it searches the directory containing the document it's displaying at that moment. As long as **morelinks.html** really is in that same directory, the browser will find it and open it.

You can make a browser look somewhere different for a file in a similar way. Open the directory containing these two documents, create a subdirectory called **pages**, and move the **morelinks.html** file into it. The link we just added now needs to be changed to the following:

> < A HREF = "pages/morelinks.html" > Here's a few more links. < /A >

The browser now looks in the current directory for another directory called **pages**, and looks inside that for **morelinks.html**.

Finally, let's open **morelinks.html** and create a link back to our original document (which we called **links.html**) so that you can click your way to and fro between the two. To do this, we need to tell the browser to look in the parent directory of **pages** to find this file: to move up one level in the directory tree, just type two dots:

> < A HREF = "../links.html" > Here's my first links page. < /A >

Case-sensitive filenames

When you refer to a page or file in your document, the case is vital. If you type in a link to Index.html and the file is actually called index.html or Index.HTML, the page won't be found. Most Web authors save all their files with lower-case names to remove any uncertainty. Similarly, although you can use long filenames, they mustn't include any spaces.

So far we've looked at linking to other Web pages, but a hyperlink needn't necessarily point to a **.html** document. If you have a movie file, a text file, a sound file, or whatever, create the link in exactly the same way, entering the location and name of this file between the double-quotes. If the file is particularly large, however, it's good practice to mention its size somewhere nearby so that people can choose whether or not to click that link.

Adding colour to the page

At this stage, in our example Web page, everything looks a bit dull. The background is white, the text is black, the hyperlinks are blue – these are the default colours set up by Internet Explorer, and it's using them because we haven't told it to use anything different. All of this is easily changed, though, by typing our preferences into that opening < BODY > tag.

This brings us to a new area of HTML. A tag like < B > is self-contained – it turns on bold text, with no complications. Other tags need to contain a little more information. A good example is the < FONT > tag, which we'll look at more closely later in this chapter. By itself, it isn't saying anything useful: which font? what size? what colour? You provide this information by adding **attributes** to the tag such as SIZE = 3, FACE = Arial, and so on, so a complete font tag might be: < FONT SIZE = 3 FACE = Arial > .

The < BODY > tag doesn't have to contain attributes, but browsers will use their own default settings for anything you haven't specified, and different browsers use different defaults. Most Web authors like to keep as much control as possible over how their pages will be displayed, and make their own settings for the body attributes. There are six attributes you can use in the < BODY > tag:

This attribute...	...has this effect
BGCOLOR =	Sets the background colour of the Web page
TEXT =	Sets the colour of text on the page
LINK =	Sets the colour of the clickable hyperlinks
VLINK =	Sets the colour of a link to a previously-visited page
ALINK =	Sets the colour of a link between the time it's clicked and the new page opening
BACKGROUND =	Specifies an image to use as the page's 'wallpaper'

Without further ado, open the original **links.html** document that you created at the start of this chapter, and change the < BODY > tag so that it looks like this:

< BODY BGCOLOR = MAROON TEXT = WHITE LINK = YELLOW VLINK = OLIVE ALINK = LIME >

Save the file, and take a look at it in your browser.
Okay, the colour scheme may not be to your taste, but
it's starting to resemble a 'real' Web page! Try
swapping colours around to find a scheme you prefer.
There are 140 colours to choose from, and you'll find a
Colour Chart included on the accompanying CD-ROM.

The other attribute is BACKGROUND = , which
places a GIF or JPEG image on the Web page, and tiles
it to fill the entire area. Let's assume you want to use
an image file called **hoops.gif** which is in the same
directory as the current document. Inside the body tag,
add: BACKGROUND = "hoops.gif" (not forgetting the
double-quotes). Your whole < BODY > tag might now
look like this:

```
< BODY BACKGROUND = "hoops.gif" BGCOLOR
    = MAROON TEXT = WHITE LINK
    = YELLOW VLINK = OLIVE ALINK = LIME >
```

Set up your font options

At the moment you're also stuck with a single font
(probably Times New Roman). Once again, this is set
up by your browser by default, and of course, different
browsers might use different default fonts. Fortunately,
the < FONT > tag leaps to your rescue, allowing you to
choose and change the font-face, size and colour
whenever you need to. Here's an example of a
< FONT > tag using all three attributes:

```
< FONT FACE = "Verdana,Arial,Helvetica" SIZE
    = 4 COLOR = RED > ... < /FONT >
```

Let's take these one at a time. The FACE attribute is
the name of the font you want to use. Obviously this
should be a font you have on your own system, but
the same font needs to be on the system of anyone
visiting your page too: if it isn't, their browser will
revert to the default font. You can keep a bit of extra
control by listing more than one font (separated by
commas) as in the example above. If the first font isn't
available, the browser will try the second, and so on.

Which fonts should I use?

Try to pick fonts that most visitors to your site will have on their systems so that they'll see the page as you intended. Most visitors to your site will have Arial and Times New Roman. Microsoft supplies a pack of fonts for the Web which many Web authors now use, including Comic Sans MS, Verdana, Impact and Georgia. You can download any of these you don't already have from **http://www.microsoft.com/truetype/fontpack/win.htm**.

Font sizes in HTML work differently than in your word-processor. There are seven sizes, numbered (unsurprisingly) from 1 to 7, where 1 is smallest. The default size for text is 3, so if you want to make your text slightly larger, use SIZE = 4. The SIZE attribute doesn't affect the headings we covered earlier, so if you've used one of these somewhere between your < FONT > and < /FONT > tags, it will still be formatted as a heading.

The colour of the text has already been set in the < BODY > tag, but you might want to slip in an occasional < FONT COLOR = PURPLE > ... < /FONT > to change the colour of a certain word, paragraph, or heading. After the closing < /FONT > tag, the colour will revert to that set in the < BODY > tag.

With the earlier changes to the < BODY > tag, and the addition of a couple of < /FONT > tags, here's what the body of our document might look like now:

```
< BODY BGCOLOR = MAROON TEXT = WHITE LINK
  = YELLOW VLINK = OLIVE ALINK = LIME >

< FONT FACE = "Comic Sans MS" COLOR = YELLOW >
< H1 > Welcome To My Homepage! < /H1 >
< /FONT >

< FONT FACE = "Arial" >
```

Here's the first paragraph.
< P > And here's the second paragraph.
< P > Visit Macromedia's snazzy < A
HREF = "http://www.macromedia.com/shockzone"
   > Shockzone < /A > site.

< /FONT >
< /BODY >
< /HTML >

Page planning with horizontal rules

Horizontal rules are straight lines that divide a page
into sections. For the simplest type of rule, the only tag
you need is < HR > . This automatically puts a
horizontal rule across the full width of the page, on a
new line, and any text that follows it will form a new
paragraph. Because the rule isn't something that needs
to be turned off again, there's no closing tag.

If you want to, you can get clever with rules by
adding some (or all!) of the attributes on the next page:

It's worth playing with the < HR > tag and its
attributes to see what unusual effects you can create.
For example, the following piece of code places a
square bullet in the centre of the page which makes a
smart, 'minimalist' divider:

< HR SIZE = 10 WIDTH = 10 COLOR = LIME
   NOSHADE >

Use this attribute...	...for this result
ALIGN =	Use LEFT or RIGHT to place the rule on the left or right of the page. If you leave this out, the rule will be centred.
SIZE =	Enter any number to set the height of the rule in pixels. The default setting is 2.
WIDTH =	Enter a number to specify the width of the line in pixels, or as a percentage of the page (such as WIDTH = 70%).
NOSHADE	This removes the 3D effect from the rule. There's no equals sign, and nothing more to add.
COLOR =	Enter the name of a colour. The default setting depends upon the background colour. Only Internet Explorer supports this attribute – other browsers will ignore it.

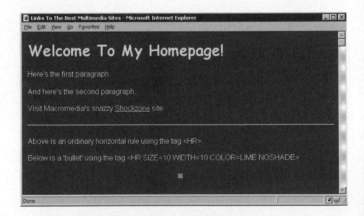

Add spice with an image

The horizontal rule is the simplest type of graphical content you can include on a page, but it's hardly exciting. To liven up a dull page, you can't go far wrong with a well-chosen image. Images on the Web are usually in either of two formats, GIF or JPEG, which are supported by almost any paint program.

Once you've chosen the image you want to use, the < IMG > tag will slot it onto the page. This tag works rather like the < FONT > tag – by itself it's meaningless, with all the information being supplied by adding attributes. Let's assume you want to insert an image called **splash.gif**, and the image file is in the same directory as your current HTML document:

    < IMG SRC = "splash.gif" >

This is the < IMG > tag at its most basic: the SRC attribute (which is short for 'source') tells the browser where to find the image file you want to display, following exactly the same rules as those for relative URLs which we looked at earlier. Unless you preceded this tag with < P > or < BR >, the image will be placed immediately after the last piece of text you entered. If you enclose the entire tag between < CENTER > and < /CENTER > tags, the image will be placed below the previous line of text, centred on the page. You do get a little more choice than that about where the image should be, though, by adding the ALIGN attribute:

This attribute...	Does this...
ALIGN = TOP	Aligns the top of the image with the top of the text on the same line.
ALIGN = MIDDLE	Aligns the middle of the image with the text on that line.
ALIGN = BOTTOM	Aligns the bottom of the image with the bottom of the line of text.
ALIGN = LEFT	Places the image on a new line, and against the left margin.
ALIGN = RIGHT	Places the image on a new line, and against the right margin.

Using these attributes, then, you can place the image roughly where you want it on the page. What's still needed is a bit of fine-tuning: after all, if you use ALIGN = MIDDLE, the image will be butted right up against the text on the same line. The answer comes in the form of two more attributes which add some blank space around an image: HSPACE = inserts space either side of the image (horizontally), and VSPACE = adds space above and below it (vertically). Just enter a number in pixels after the equals sign. As usual with attributes, if you only need to use one of these, there's no need to include the other. So an image might be inserted with a tag that looks like this:

    < IMG SRC = "splash.gif" ALIGN = MIDDLE
    HSPACE = 30 VSPACE = 6 >

Use an image as an anchor

Earlier in this chapter you learnt how to create hypertext links, or anchors, to a Web page or file using the tag **< A HREF = "*URL*" >** *clickable text* **< /A >** . But the clickable section that appears on the page doesn't have to be text: you can use an image instead, or both image and text. For example, if you slot the whole image tag given above into the anchor tag, the image will appear exactly as it did before, but will now act as a clickable link:

    < A HREF = "morelinks.html" > < IMG SRC
    = "splash.gif" ALIGN = MIDDLE HSPACE =
    30 VSPACE = 6 WIDTH = 84 HEIGHT =
    81 BORDER = 0 > < /A > Click this image to open
    my other links page.

To make both the text and the image clickable, add some text before or after the < IMG > tag like this:

    < A HREF = "morelinks.html" > Click this image to
    open my other links page. < IMG
SRC = "splash.gif"
    ALIGN = MIDDLE HSPACE = 30 VSPACE =

6 WIDTH = 84 HEIGHT = 81 BORDER = 0 > < /A >

Here's what those two methods look like when displayed in your browser:

Glossary

Arriving on the Internet is a bit like arriving in a foreign country – suddenly everyone around you seems to be talking a different language. This is the part of the book that helps you to find out what they're all on about, or even to learn to speak like a native yourself.

Yes, it's all the technical stuff, but we'll keep it as painless as possible. Keep a look out for words and phrases in italic text – they indicate a related entry.

access provider A general term for a company that lets you connect to the *Internet* by dialling in to their computer in return for money. This may be an *Internet Access Provider* or an *online service*.

ActiveX A new multimedia programming system developed by Microsoft for use on the *World Wide Web*.

alias A nifty short name for something whose real name is much longer. For example, your *email* software will usually let you refer to yourself as Joe Bloggs instead of j_bloggs@somewhere.co.uk.

animated GIF A type of animation created by loading two or more *GIF* images into an animation program, setting an order and delay times and re-saving as a single file.

anonymous FTP A method of getting access to files on an *FTP* site without needing special permission or a *logon* name. Instead you enter **anonymous** as your logon name, and your email address as your password.

anonymous remailers Services that will forward your *email* messages or newsgroup *articles* after stripping out your personal details, so that no-one can tell who sent them.

Archie A system that lets you track down files on *FTP* sites by entering the name of the file (or part of it) into a program that can search through indexes of files on these computers.

article For no particularly good reason, the name for a message sent to a *newsgroup*.

archive A single file which usually contains several (or many) other files to make for quicker and easier *downloading*. Most archives also compress these files into a smaller space than they'd ordinarily take up, speeding up downloads still further.

ASCII Pronounced 'ass-key', and often referred to as **plain text**. This is a text system that allows ordinary numbers and letters, punctuation marks such as spaces, tabs and carriage-returns, plus a few special characters, but no formatting or font information. ASCII text can be recognised by almost any type of computer and read in any word-processor.

attachments Files included with a message to be sent by *email* or to a *newsgroup*. Messages that contain attachments are indicated by a paper-clip icon in most software.

attributes In *HTML*, these are additions to tags that let you specify or change what the tag should do. For example, <HR> creates a rule across the page. Adding the WIDTH= and ALIGN= attributes lets you create a short rule placed on the left side of the page.

bandwidth A general term for the amount of information that can be transferred over an Internet connection. Often used in terms of 'wasting bandwidth' by, for example, sending the same *article* to 30 different *newsgroups* when it was only relevant to one.

BBS (Bulletin Board System) A computer which provides an *email* service and file archives (and perhaps more) which members can connect to via a *modem*. Some online services such as CompuServe started life as BBSs before becoming connected to the *Internet*.

binaries or **binary files** The term for a file that contains anything but plain *ASCII* text (such as a program, movie, or formatted document). Also appears in *newsgroup* names to indicate that non-text files can be attached to articles in the group.

bookmarks The Netscape Navigator name for *Favorites*.

bounced email *Email* messages that come back to you instead of being delivered, usually because you typed the *email address* wrongly.

browser The vital piece of *Internet* software, ostensibly designed for viewing pages from the *World Wide Web*, but capable of handling almost all of your Internet activities. The two most popular browsers are Microsoft's Internet Explorer, and Netscape's Navigator.

cache A directory on your own system into which your *browser* stores all the files it *downloads* from the *World Wide Web* in case you want to view those pages again – it can then load them quickly from this directory instead of downloading them all over again.

chat A type of conversation which takes place by typing messages back and forth instead of speaking (other than to swear at the chat software). A popular chat system is *IRC*, but online services have their own chat rooms, and other software allows one-to-one chatting by 'dialling-up' an *email address* rather like using a telephone.

client The name for something (usually a software program) that makes use of a service. For example, your *email* program is a client that makes use of the email service. The opposite term is *server*.

compressed files see *archive*

containers The name for the type of tags used in *HTML* that must have a closing tag (such as < B > ... < /B > for bold text). The text to which the tags are being applied is contained within them.

cookies Small text files that some *Web sites* store on your computer so that they know who you are next time you visit.

cyberspace A word coined by William Gibson in his novel 'Neuromancer'. It's used as a very generalised term for the *Internet* and everything that comes with it.

Dial-Up Networking The *TCP/IP stack* built into Microsoft Windows 95, Windows NT 4.0, and later operating systems, that makes setting up an *Internet* connection a relatively pain-free task.

DNS see *Domain Name System*

domain name This is the name given to a computer on the *Internet* that's (vaguely) recognisable to human beings, such as **www.royalnetwork.com**. Every computer on the Net has its own unique name.

Domain Name System (DNS) Also defined as Domain Name Server. This system translates the friendly *domain names* that we humans like to work with into the *IP addresses* that computers like to work with.

dot address Another name for *IP address*.

downloading The act of copying files (of any type) to your own computer from some other computer. The opposite term is *uploading*.

email or **e-mail** Short for 'electronic mail', a system that lets you send text messages over a *network* from one computer to another.

email address An address consisting of your *username* and the host name of your service provider's computer, in the form **username@host**. Because this host name is unique, and you're the only subscriber with that username, the email address is as personal to you as your phone number.

emoticons Little pictures (usually faces) made out of typed characters and viewed sideways-on, such as :-) meaning Happy.

encryption The term for altering data or text to turn it into meaningless gobbledegook. Only someone with the correct decoding information (or 'key') can read and use it.

FAQ (Frequently Asked Questions) A list of questions and answers on a particular subject. These are frequently placed in *newsgroups* so that the group doesn't become bogged down with new users asking the same questions all the time. You'll also find FAQs on Web sites, and almost anywhere else in the computing world.

Favorites A menu in Microsoft's Internet Explorer *browser* (and a corresponding directory on your hard disk) containing shortcuts to sites that you visit regularly. You can revisit a site easily by clicking its name on the menu, and add new sites to the menu with a couple of clicks.

FTP (File Transfer Protocol) One of the many *protocols* used to copy files from one computer to another on the *Internet*. Also used in terms like 'an FTP site' (a site that lets you grab files from it using this protocol), and as a verb, as in 'You can ftp to this site'.

Finger A command (or a software program that sends the command) which returns information about someone whose *email address* you entered. Also used as a verb, so this is one instance in which you can 'finger' someone and get away with it.

flame A negative or abusive response to a *newsgroup article* or an *email* message.

follow-up A reply to an *email* or *newsgroup* message that contains the same subject line (prefixed with RE) and continues the same *thread*.

freeware Software that you don't have to pay for.

gateway A program or device that acts as a kind of translator between two *networks* that wouldn't otherwise be able to communicate with each other.

GIF One of the two major graphics formats used on the *Internet* (along with *JPEG*). GIF images can be saved with between 2 and 256 colours, so they contain less information than the 16-million-colour JPEG format, and therefore make smaller files. They're suitable for anything but photographs and the most lifelike art. See also *animated GIFs*.

Gopher A menu-based system for storing, searching for, and retrieving documents, which was the precursor to the *World Wide Web*.

history list A list of recently-visited sites stored by your *browser* so that you can see where you've been, get back there easily or find out what someone else has been using your browser for.

homepage Two definitions for this one. 1. The page displayed in your *browser* when you first run it, or when you click the Home button. 2. The first page (or main contents page) of a *Web site*.

host A computer connected directly (and usually permanently) to the *Internet* that allows other computers to connect to it (like your service provider's computer). This also leads to the expression 'host name' which means the same as *domain name*.

HTML see *Hypertext Markup Language*

HTTP (HyperText Transfer Protocol) The *protocol* used to transfer Web pages around the *Internet*, along with the images and other ingredients that go with them.

hypertext A system of clickable text used on the *World Wide Web*, as well as in older Windows help files and CD-ROM-based encyclopaedias. A hypertext *link* can be inserted wherever a cross-reference to another part of the document (or an entirely different document) is needed.

Hypertext Markup Language (HTML) A fairly simple system of textual codes that can be added to an *ASCII* text file to turn it into a Web page.

IAP see *Internet Access Provider*

Internet Often shortened to just 'the Net'. The Internet is a gigantic *network* of computers, all linked together and able to exchange information. No-one owns or controls it, and anyone can connect to it. Without the capital 'I', an internet is a more general term for networks connected to each other.

Internet Access Provider (IAP) A company that allows anyone to connect to the *Internet* by dialling into their host computer. All they ask in return is that you give them money. Also sometimes referred to as an Internet Service Provider, or ISP.

Internet Protocol (IP) see *TCP/IP*

IP Address (Internet Protocol Address) Every computer on the *Internet* has its own unique address, which can appear in two forms: the friendlier *domain name*, or as an IP address that computers themselves use. This consists of four numbers separated by dots, such as 148.159.6.26. Also known as a 'dot address'.

IRC (Internet Relay Chat) An *Internet* service that provides one of the most popular *chat* systems which can be accessed using many different IRC programs. Chat rooms in IRC are referred to as 'channels'.

ISDN An abbreviation for Integrated Services Digital Network. An ISDN line allows faster access to the *Internet* than current modems allow, and can simultaneously handle voice and data.

ISP (Internet Service Provider) see *Internet Access Provider*

Java A software-programming language developed by Sun MicroSystems Inc. The language is often used to write small programs called 'applets' that can be inserted in a Web page.

JavaScript A similar language to *Java*, except that it's written in plain text and can be inserted 'as is' into a *HTML* document to place effects or small programs on a Web page.

JPEG Along with *GIF*, this is one of the two most-used formats for images on the Net. This format saves information for 16.7 million colours, making it ideal for photographs but creating unnecessarily large files for most forms of artwork.

leased line A line leased from the telephone company that provides a permanent, dedicated connection to an *Internet Access Provider*. Leased lines are lightning fast and cost a small fortune. (Also known as a 'T1 connection'.)

link As a noun, a link is a piece of clickable *hypertext*, identifiable by being underlined and a different colour from the ordinary text around it. As a verb, to link to a site or page means the same as to open or *download* it.

log off A synonym for 'disconnect' – logging off means telling the computer you're connected to that you've finished for this session.

log on/logon Either of these can be used as a noun or a verb. When you log on to a service or computer you are identifying yourself, usually by entering a *username* and password. This act may be referred to as 'a logon', or 'logging on'. Your username may be termed a 'logon name'.

lurking A cute term for observing something without taking an active rôle. This may refer to visiting chat rooms and just following conversations rather than chatting, or reading *newsgroups* without *posting* any *articles* yourself.

mailing list This can mean two things. 1. A list of *email addresses* to which you can send the same message without making endless copies of it, all with different addresses inserted. 2. A discussion group similar to *newsgroups*, but all the messages sent to the group are forwarded to its members by email.

mail server A computer (or program) dedicated to transferring email messages around the *Internet*. This might be referred to as an *SMTP* server or a *POP3* server.

MIME (Multipurpose Internet Mail Extensions) A method of organising different types of file by assigning each its own 'MIME type'. Most of the *Internet* software you use can recognise these types and determine what to do with a file it receives (or ask you how you want to treat it). MIME is used to handle *attachments* in *email* and *newsgroup* messages, as well as files found on Web pages.

mirror site An exact copy of a site located on a different computer. Many popular sites have one or more mirrors around the world so that users can connect to the site nearest to them, thus easing the load on the main computer.

modem An acronym formed from the words 'modulator' and 'demodulator'. A modem converts data back and forth between the format recognised by computers and the format needed to send it down telephone lines.

MPEG Along with *QuickTime*, one of the two most popular formats for movie files on the *Internet*, requiring an MPEG player and (ideally) special hardware for playback.

MUD (Multi User Dungeon) A type of text-based adventure game that might be played by a single user, or by multiple users adopting characters and 'chatting' by typing messages.

netiquette An amalgamation of the words 'Internet' and 'etiquette' that refers to good behaviour on the Net. Netiquette essentially boils down to two rules: avoid offensive comments and actions and don't waste *Internet* resources (or *bandwidth*).

network Two or more computers that are connected to each other (or can be connected via telephone lines and *modems*) and can pass information back and forth.

newbie A colloquial name for someone new to the *Internet*, or to a particular area of it, and is perhaps prone to a bit of fumbling around. Although a slightly derogatory term, it's not meant to be offensive – you might describe yourself as a newbie when appealing for help.

newsgroup A discussion group with a particular topic in which users leave messages for others to read and reply to. There are almost 30,000 such groups, and many more *mailing lists* which follow similar methods. Newsgroups are sometimes referred to as Usenet groups.

newsreader The software program that you use to access *newsgroups*, and to read, send and reply to *articles*.

news server A computer (or program) dedicated to transferring the contents of *newsgroups* around the Net, and to and from your computer. This might be referred to as an *NNTP* server.

NNTP (Network News Transfer Protocol) One of many *protocols* used on the Net to transfer information around. This particular protocol handles messages from *newsgroups*.

offline A synonym for 'not connected'. In Net terms, being offline is generally a good thing (unless you're trying and failing to get *online*): the ability to compose messages offline and send them all in a bunch later, or view *downloaded* files offline, can save you money in connection charges.

online A synonym for 'connected'. Anything connected to your computer and ready for action can be said to be online. In *Internet* terms, it means that you've successfully dialled in to your service provider's computer and are now connected to the Net. The opposite term is *offline*.

online service A members-only service that allows users to join discussion groups (or 'forums'), exchange *email* messages with other members, download files and a fair bit more besides. Most popular online services (such as America Online and CompuServe) are now connected to the *Internet* as well.

packet The name for a unit of data being sent across the Net. A system called 'packet switching' breaks a file up into packets, marks each with the addresses of the sending and receiving computers and sends each packet off individually. These packets may arrive at your computer via different routes and in the wrong order, but your computer uses the extra information they contain to piece the file back together.

PING (Packet InterNet Groper) The name of a command (or a program that sends a command) that tests a connection between two computers. It does this by sending a tiny amount of data to a specified computer and noting how long it takes to reply. (The reply, incidentally, is called a PONG.)

plug-in An add-on program for a *browser* that can play or display a certain type of file in the browser's own window.

PoP (Point of Presence) An unnecessarily technical name for a phone number you can dial to connect to your service provider's computer. Many service providers have PoPs all over the country; others cater just for the major cities or a single small area.

POP3 (Post Office Protocol) One of two *protocols* (along with *SMTP*) used to transfer *email* messages around the Net. POP is used for receiving email, and lets you collect your messages from any computer you happen to be using. The '3' refers to the latest version of the protocol.

posting When you send an email message, the word 'sending' is quite good enough. When you send a message to a *newsgroup*, it isn't. Instead, for no adequately explained reason, the word 'posting' is used.

PGP (Pretty Good Privacy) A popular, but complicated, system of *encryption*.

PPP (Point to Point Protocol) A *protocol* used to connect computers to the Internet via a telephone line and a modem. It's similar to *SLIP*, but more recent and easier to set up.

protocol A type of 'language' that two computers agree to speak when they need to communicate and don't speak each other's native language. In other words, a sort of Esperanto for computers, but networking and *Internet* connections use a great many different protocols to do different things.

QuickTime Along with *MPEG*, this is one of the most popular movie file formats on the Net, developed by Apple. To view these files you'll need the QuickTime Viewer. There is also a virtual reality version (QuickTime VR) which is gaining in popularity.

RealAudio The most popular format for *streaming* audio on the Net, requiring the RealAudio Player (included with Internet Explorer) for playback.

refresh (or **reload**) Forcing the *browser* to *download* a Web page again by clicking a toolbar button labelled Refresh (in Internet Explorer) or Reload (in Netscape Navigator). You might do this to make sure you're looking at the latest version of a page, or as an attempt to get things moving again if the page began to download and everything ground to a halt.

rot13 (rotated 13) A simple method used to *encrypt email* and *newsgroup* messages so that you won't accidentally read something that might offend you.

search engine A Web site that maintains an index of other Web pages and sites, allowing you to search for pages on a particular subject by entering keywords. Because these engines gather their information in different ways, you can get markedly varying results from using different search sites.

server A computer or program that provides a service to a *client*. For example, your email client (the program that lets you work with *email* messages) connects to your service provider's mail server when you decide to send or receive your email.

service provider A general term for a company that gives you access to the *Internet* by letting you dial in to their computer. This may be an *Internet Access Provider* or an *online service*.

shareware A system for selling software that lets you try before you buy. If you like the program, you pay for it. If you don't, you stop using it and delete it from your system.

signature A short piece of text you can create that gets appended to your *email* and *newsgroup* messages when you send them. This might give contact information (perhaps your name, email address, company name, etc.), a neat little phrase or quote, or perhaps an elaborate piece of *ASCII* art (rather like an *emoticon*, but bigger).

SLIP (Serial Line Internet Protocol) A similar *protocol* to *PPP*, but older and best avoided (especially if you use Windows 95, Windows NT 4.0 or later).

smiley see *emoticon*

SMTP (Simple Mail Transfer Protocol) Along with *POP3*, one of the two protocols that are used to transfer *email* messages around the Net. SMTP can be used to both send and receive messages, but POP3 has more flexibility for receiving. When POP3 is being used, SMTP simply handles the sending of messages.

source The name for the *HTML* document that forms a Web page, containing all the tags that determine what your *browser* should display, and how. You can look at the source for a Web page in Internet Explorer by clicking the View menu and selecting Source.

spamming A Net jargon term for sending the same message to multiple *newsgroups* or *email* recipients regardless of their interest (or lack of it). Most spamming consists of unsolicited advertisements. Apart from the personal aggravation it causes, spamming is also a massive waste of *bandwidth*.

streaming Some of the latest formats for video and audio on the Net allow the file to play while it's being *downloaded*, rather than forcing you to wait for the entire file to download first.

tags The name for the *HTML* codes added to a plain *ASCII* document which turn it into a Web page with full formatting and links to other files and pages.

talk A talk program lets you speak to someone elsewhere in the world using your *modem* and *Internet* connection instead of your telephone. You need a soundcard and microphone, and the other person must be using the same program as you. Also known as Voice On the Net (VON). The term 'talk' is also used to describe the kind of typed chat that takes place between two people rather than a group in a chat room.

TCP/IP (Transmission Control Protocol/Internet Protocol) Two vital *protocols* that work together to handle communications between your computer and the rest of the *Internet*.

TCP/IP Stack For a computer to connect to the *Internet*, it must have a TCP/IP stack, which consists of *TCP/IP* software, *packet* driver software, and sockets software. Windows 95 and later Windows operating systems come with their own TCP/IP stack called *Dial-Up Networking*. In Windows 3x, the TCP/IP stack has to be installed separately: one of the best stacks is Trumpet Winsock. (See also *Winsock*.)

Telnet A program that allows *Internet* users to connect to a distant computer and control it through their own computer. Nowadays the main use of Telnet is in playing games like *MUDs*.

thread An ongoing topic of conversation in a *newsgroup* or *mailing list*. When someone posts a message with a new Subject line they're starting a new thread. Any replies to this message (and replies to replies, and so on) will have the same Subject line and continue the thread.

TLAs (Three Letter Acronyms) Not necessarily acronyms, and not necessarily three letters either, but TLAs are a type of shorthand for common phrases that are used in conversation and messages on the Net, such as BTW for 'By the way', FAQ for 'Frequently asked question' and KISS for 'Keep it simple, stupid'

Transmission Control Protocol (TCP) see *TCP/IP*

uploading The term for copying files from your own computer to a distant computer, usually by using *FTP*. The opposite term is *downloading*.

URL (Uniform Resource Locator) (Pronounced 'earl'.) The unique 'address' of a file on the Internet consisting of a *protocol* (such as http://), a computer name (such as www.computer.co.uk) and a path to the file on that computer (such as /public/files/program.zip).

Usenet A large network that distributes many of the Net's *newsgroups*.

username A unique name you're assigned by a service that enables you to *log on* to it and identify yourself, demonstrating that you're entitled to access it. When you set up your *Internet* access account, your username will usually form part of your *email address* too.

Uuencode/Uudecode To send computer files in *email* or *newsgroup* messages, they have to be converted to plain *ASCII* text first. Uuencoding is a system for converting files this way; Uudecoding converts the text back into a file at the other end. Special software may be needed to do this, but many email and newsgroup programs have built-in automatic Uuencode/Uudecode facilities.

VBScript A scripting language developed by Microsoft, similar to *JavaScript*.

Veronica An acronym for 'Very Easy Rodent-Oriented Net-wide Index to Computerised Archives'. Veronica is a facility built into *Gopher* that allows searching for files on gopher sites.

viewer A program used to view, play or display files that you find on the Net. Unlike a *plug-in*, a viewer will open the file in its own separate window. Because it's a stand-alone program, you can also use it *offline* to view files already on your own system.

virus A small program created by a warped mind that can use various methods to attach itself to programs. When the program is run, so is the virus. A virus might do no more harm to your system than making it go beep occasionally, or it might trash all your data and even make your computer unusable. The main risk of 'catching' a virus comes from using programs on a floppy disk of unknown origin or *downloaded* from the *Internet* without first running them through virus-checker software.

Voice On the Net (VON) see *talk*

VRML (Virtual Reality Modelling Language) A language used to build 3-dimensional models and 'worlds' that you can view using special software.

WAIS (Wide Area Information Server) A little-used service for searching databases of information on the Net.

Web see *World Wide Web*

Web page A single document (usually having the extension .htm or .html) forming a tiny part of the *World Wide Web*, often containing text, images, and *links* to other pages and files on the Web. To view Web pages you need a *browser*.

Web server A computer or program dedicated to storing *Web pages* and transmitting them to your computer to be viewed in your *browser*.

Web site A collection of related *Web pages* and files, usually created by or belonging to a single individual or company, and located on the same *Web server*.

Web space Usually refers to space on a *Web server* provided to *Internet* users so that they can create and publish their own *Web sites*. This space may be provided free, or for a monthly charge.

Whois A command (or a program which can send the command) that can find someone's *email* address and other information about them based on the name entered.

Winsock Abbreviation of Windows Sockets, the sockets software program for Windows operating systems called Winsock.dll, that forms the basis of a *TCP/IP stack*.

World Wide Web A vast collection of documents and files stored on Web servers. The documents are known as *Web pages* and are created using a language called *HTML*. All these pages and files are linked together using a system of *hypertext*.

Directory

1: UK Internet Access Providers

Use the list below to find an IAP with the services you're looking for, then give them a ring, ask about pricing and check some of the other details mentioned in Chapter 2.

All the IAPs noted here offer full UK coverage and the basic services of email, World Wide Web, FTP, Telnet, Gopher, IRC and newsgroup access.

Bear in mind that this isn't an exhaustive list, and these details change regularly – for example, more and more IAPs are starting to offer free Web-space – so it doesn't hurt to ask if the details don't exactly match what you want. Most IAPs have special packages for business users and other connection options available.

Company:	**ACE**		*Company:*	**Almac**
Telephone:	01670 528204		*Telephone:*	01324 666336
Email:	info@ace.co.uk		*Email:*	info@almac.co.uk
WWW Site:	www.ace.co.uk		*WWW Site:*	www.almac.co.uk
Notes:	Free Web-space		*Notes:*	Free Web-space; FTP archive; free demo service

Company:	**Aspen Internet**
Telephone:	01672 511290
Email:	admin@aspen-internet.net
WWW Site:	www.aspen-internet.net
Notes:	PPP; POP3 email; domain registration

Company:	**BT Internet (British Telecom)**
Telephone:	0800 800001
Email:	info@bt.net
WWW Site:	www.btinternet.com
Notes:	Free Web-space; POP3 email

Company:	**CityScape**
Telephone:	01223 566950
Email:	sales@cityscape.co.uk
WWW Site:	www.cityscape.co.uk
Notes:	Free Web-space; POP3 email; FTP archive

Company:	**Demon Internet**
Telephone:	0181-371 1234
Email:	sales@demon.net
WWW Site:	www.demon.net
Notes:	PPP; POP3 email; FTP archive; free demo available

Company:	**Direct Connection**
Telephone:	0181-297 2200
Email:	sales@dircon.co.uk
WWW Site:	www.dircon.co.uk
Notes:	PPP; POP3 email; free demo available

Company:	**Direct Net @ccess**
Telephone:	01232 330311
Email:	info@d-n-a.net
WWW Site:	www.d-n-a.net
Notes:	3 email addresses; free Web-space

Company:	**Easynet**
Telephone:	0171-209 0990
Email:	admin@easynet.co.uk
WWW Site:	www.easynet.co.uk
Notes:	Free Web-space

Company:	**Enterprise**
Telephone:	01624 677666
Email:	sales@enterprise.net
WWW Site:	www.enterprise.net
Notes:	PPP; Web and FTP space

Company:	**Global Internet**
Telephone:	0181-957 1005
Email:	info@globalnet.co.uk
WWW Site:	www.globalnet.co.uk
Notes:	PPP; Web-space available

Company:	**Hiway**
Telephone:	01635 550660
Email:	info@inform.hiway.co.uk
WWW Site:	www.hiway.co.uk
POPs:	UK coverage
Notes:	POP3 email; free Web-space; FTP archive and space

Company:	**Netforce Group**
Telephone:	01245 257788
Email:	sales@netforce.net
WWW Site:	www.netforce.net
Notes:	PPP; Web and FTP space available; FTP archive

Company:	**.netKonect**
Telephone:	01420 542777
Email:	info@netkonect.net
WWW Site:	www.netkonect.net
Notes:	Web-space available

Company:	Nildram		Company:	Talk-101
Telephone:	0800 072 0400		Telephone:	01925 245145
Email:	info@nildram.co.uk		Email:	sales@talk-101.com
WWW Site:	www.nildram.co.uk		WWW Site:	www.talk-101/com
Notes:	PPP; FTP & Web-space		Notes:	PPP; FTP & Web space

Company:	Onyx Internet		Company:	Total Connectivity Providers
Telephone:	0345 715715		Telephone.	01703 393392
Email:	sales@onyxnet.co.uk		Email:	sales@tcp.co.uk
WWW Site:	www.onyxnet.co.uk		WWW Site:	www.tcp.co.uk
Notes:	Web-space available		Notes:	PPP; POP3 email; Web-space; free trial

Company.	Primex Information Services			
Telephone:	07000 774639		Company:	U-NET
Email.	info@alpha.primex.co.uk		Telephone:	01925 484444
WWW Site:	www.primex.co.uk		Email:	hi@u-net.com
Notes:	PPP; Web space; various subscriptions available		WWW Site:	www.u-net.com
			Notes:	PPP; POP3 email; Web-space

Company:	Rednet			
Telephone:	01494 513333		Company:	Unipalm Pipex
Email:	info@rednet.co.uk		Telephone:	01223 250100
WWW Site:	www.rednet.co.uk		Email:	sales@pipex.net
Notes:	PPP; free Web-space; POP3 email		WWW Site:	www.unipalm.pipex.com
			Notes:	PPP; free Web-space

Company:	Sonnet Internet		Company:	Zetnet Services
Telephone:	0171-891 2000		Telephone:	01595 696667
Email:	enquire@sonnet.co.uk		Email:	info@zetnet.co.uk
WWW Site:	www.sonnet.co.uk		WWW Site:	www.zetnet.co.uk
Notes:	PPP; Web-space		Notes:	Free Web-space; free trial

2: UK online services

The following is a list of the online services available. If you don't have the free software required to subscribe, give them a call and ask for it.

Most services offer several different subscription schemes that include varying amounts of 'free' online time per month, or unlimited access for a higher monthly fee. Don't forget to find out what your options are or your online time could end up costing you far more than it needs to!

America Online (AOL)

Telephone:	0800 279 1234
Email:	queryuk@aol.com
WWW Site:	www.aol.com
POPs:	UK coverage

CIX

Telephone:	0181-2969666
Email:	sales@compulink.co.uk
WWW Site:	www.compulink.co.uk
POPs:	UK coverage

ClaraNET

Telephone:	0171-647 1000
Email:	sales@clara.net
WWW Site:	www.clara.net
POPs:	UK coverage

CompuServe Information Service

Telephone:	0800 289378
Email:	70006.101@compuserve.com
WWW Site:	www.compuserve.com
POPs:	UK coverage

Delphi Internet

Telephone:	0171-757 7080
Email:	ukservice@delphi.com
WWW Site:	www.delphi.co.uk
POPs:	London (UK coverage via GNS Network)

Microsoft Network (MSN)

Telephone:	0345 002000
WWW Site:	www.msn.com
POPs:	UK coverage

Virgin Net

Telephone:	0500 558800
Email:	mail-hq@virgin.net
WWW Site:	www.virgin.net
POPs:	UK coverage

3: UK software companies

Company	Telephone
Adobe Systems	0181-606 4000
Aldus	0131 451 6888
Andromeda Interactive	01235 529595
Attica Cybernetics	01865 200892
Autodesk	01483 303322
Avalon	01624 627227
Borland	01734 320022
Broderbund	01753 620909
Brooklyn North Software Works	0500 284177
Central Point International	01628 788580
Claris	0181-756 0101
Corel	0800 581028
Delrina	0181-207 7033
Digital Workshop	01295 258335
Dorling Kindersley	0171-753 3488
Electronic Arts	01753 549442
Gold Disk	01753 832383
Gremlin Games	0114 275 3423
GSP	01480 496789
Guildsoft	01752 895100
Health Perfect	0181-200 8897
IBM Software Enquiries	01329 242728
Interplay	01235 821666
Intuit	0181-990 5500
Lotus Development	01784 455455
Macromedia	0181-358 5857
Micrografx	0800 626009
MicroProse	01454 329510
Microsoft	01734 270001
Mirage	01260 299909
MoneyBox Software	01392 429424
Ocean	0161-839 0999
Pegasus Software	01536 495000
Psygnosis	0151-282 3000
Quark Systems	01483 454397
Quarterdeck UK	01245 494940

Company	Telephone
Sage	0191-255 3000
S&S International	01296 318700
Serif	0800 24925
Softkey	0181-789 2000
SoftQuad	0181-236 1001
Starfish Software	0181-875 4455
Symantec	01628 592222
TopLevel Computing	01453 753944
Wang UK	0181-568 9200

4: UK hardware companies

Company	Telephone	Products
AMD	01256 603121§	Processors
Apricot Computers	0121-717 7171	PCs
Brother UK	0161 330 6531	Printers
Compaq	0181-332 3888	PCs, Notebook PCs
Conner	01294 315333	Hard drives
Creative Labs	01734 344322	Soundcards, Multimedia peripherals
Cyrix	0800 137305	Processors
Diamond Multimedia	01753 501400	Display adapters, Multimedia peripherals
Epson UK	01442 227478	Printers
Fujitsu	0181-573 4444	Hard drives, Printers, Scanners
Hayes	01252 775533	Modems
Hercules	01635 861122	Display adapters
Hewlett-Packard	01344 369369	Printers
Hitachi	0181-849 2087	CD-ROM drives, Monitors
IBM	0345 500900	PCs, Notebook PCs
Iiyama	01438 745482	Monitors
Intel	01793 431144	Processors
Iomega	0800 898563	Archive and backup drives
IPC Corp UK	01282 618866	PCs, Notebook PCs, Peripherals
JVC	0181-896 6000	CD-ROM drives
Kodak	01734 311500	Printers
Lexmark International	01628 488200	Printers
Logitech	01344 891313	Mice, Trackballs, Scanners

Company	Telephone	Products
Matrox	01793 614002	Display adapters
Microsoft	01734 271000	Mice, Trackballs, Keyboards
Microvitec	01274 390011	Monitors
Mitsumi	01276 29029	CD-ROM drives
NEC Computer Products	0181-993 8111	PCs, CD-ROM drives
Nikon	0181-541 4440	Scanners
Olivetti	0800 447799	PCs, Notebook PCs, Printers
Orchid Europe	01256 844899	Display adapters
Packard Bell	0800 314314	PCs
Panasonic	01344 853508	Monitors, Printers, CD-ROM drives
Pioneer	01753 789731	CD-ROM drives
Plasmon Data	01763 262963	Recordable CD drives
Primax	01235 536374	Scanners
Psion	0171-258 7376	Palmtop computers
Roland UK	01792 702701	Soundcards, MIDI hardware
Seagate	01628 474532	Hard drives
Sony UK	0181-784 1144	CD-ROM drives, Monitors
Star Micronics	01494 471111	Printers
Toshiba	01932 785666	CD-ROM drives, Printers, Notebook PCs
Trust Peripherals	01376 500770	Scanners, modems, multimedia peripherals
US Robotics	01734 228200	Modems
VideoLogic	01923 271300	Display adapters
Visioneer	0181-358 5850	Scanners
Western Digital UK	01372 360055	Hard drives

5: UK retailers

Company	Telephone	Products
Byte Direct	0121-766 2565	PCs, Peripherals
Choice Peripherals	01909 530 242	Peripherals, Components, Software
Currys	01442 888000	PCs, Peripherals
Dabs Direct	0800 558866	PCs, Peripherals, Software, Components, Consumables
Dan Technology	0181-830 1100	PCs
Dart Computers	01794 511505	PCs
Dell	0500 500111	PCs

Company	Telephone	Products
Dixons	01442 888000	PCs, Peripherals, Software, Consumables
Elonex	0181-452 6666	PCs, Notebook PCs
Fox Computers	01621 744500	PCs, Peripherals, Components
Gateway 2000	0800 342000	PCs, Notebook PCs
Memory Bank	0181-956 7000	Memory, Peripherals, Software, Components
Mesh Computers	0181-452 1111	PCs
MrPC	01282 777888	PCs, Peripherals, Software
Multimedia Direct	01635 873000	Multimedia hardware
Novatech	0800 777500	PCs, Peripherals, Software, Consumables
PC World	0990 464464	PCs, Peripherals, Software, Consumables
Pico Direct	01483 202022	Notebook PCs, Notebook peripherals
Plug & Play Technology	0181-341 3336	PC Cards, Notebook peripherals
Roldec	01902 456464	Peripherals, Components
Silica Systems	0181-309 1111	PCs, Peripherals, Software
Simply Computers	0181-498 2130	PCs, Peripherals, Components
SMC Computers	01753 550333	PCs, Peripherals, Components
Software Warehouse	01675 466467	Software, Peripherals, Components, Consumables
Stak Trading	01788 577497	PCs, Peripherals, Components
Taurus Component Shop	01978 312372	Components, Peripherals
Tech Direct	0181-286 2222	Notebook PCs, Printers/ Peripherals, Consumables
The Link	01442 888000	PCs, Peripherals
Technomatic	0181-205 9558	PCs, Peripherals, Software, Components
Time Computer Systems	01282 777111	PCs
Tiny Computers	01293 821333	PCs
Viglen	0181-759 7000	PCs, Notebook PCs
Virgin Megastore	0171-631 1234	Software
Watford Electronics	01582 745555	PCs, Software, Peripherals, Components

6: UK general services

Data transfer, conversion, duplication

Company	Telephone
A.L.Downloading Services	0181-994 5471
Mapej	01691 778659

Data recovery (disk failure, corruption, viruses)

Company	Telephone
Authentic Data Recovery	0800 581263
Ontrack Data Recovery	0800 243996
Vogon International	01734 890042

PC rental

Company	Telephone
MC Rentals	01952 604411
Micro-Rent	0171-700 4848
Skylake Rentals	0800 373118

PC security/anti-theft

Company	Telephone
Datamark Security	01494 434757
Secure PC	0171-610 3646

PC memory

Company	Telephone
AW Computer Memory Bargains	01382 643739
Click	0800 666500
Mem Com	0161-427 2222
Mr Memory	01483 799410
Offtek	0121-722 3993

Printer consumables

Company	Telephone
Cartridge Express	01765 690790
Inkwell Direct	01344 843444
Jetica	0800 614153
Laser Printer Technologies	01482 656630
Mannink	01462 455651
Owl Associates	01543 250377
Squire International	0181-886 3078
Themis	01883 3330333
Vectorjet	01763 273115

Floppy disks

Company	Telephone
Owl Associates	01543 250377
Product Trade & Services	0800 136502
Squire International	0181-886 3078

Specialist suppliers

Company	Telephone	Products
BBD Dust Covers	01257 425839	Computer dust-covers
C&T	0171-637 1767	Storage hardware
Capital Litho	01386 40321	Personalised mouse mats
Linefeed	0171-474 1765	CD writers & media
MJ Communications	07000 663367	Modems
Monitor Man	01453 885599	Monitors
Semaphore Systems	0171-625 7744	Components
The Keyboard Company	07000 102105	Keyboards
The Monitor Shop	01159 110366	Monitors

Shareware

Company	Telephone
AWII Computer Services	01563 850645
Demon Shareware	01325 301849
Ferrari Software	01843 865083
Hornesoft PD	01142 967825
Islander Software	0345 660429
MicroWorld	01425 610699
Telescan	01253 829292

Bulletin board services *(premium rate charges apply)*

Company	Telephone
BBS Elite	0891 518299
Café Net	0891 615010
Komputer Knowledge	0891 515066
Mainline BBS	0891 615795
MegaDownLoad	0891 516126
Microland Bulletin Board	0891 990505
Strangeways BBS	0891 408040

Index

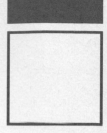

Exploring the Internet can be a confusing experience at first. Virgin Net is here to provide a helping hand – we will guide you through the pitfalls and help you get the best from the Internet. To go online, just follow these three easy steps:

If you feel yourself getting into trouble, please call our local call rate 24-hour helpline: 0845 650 0000

1. Install

You will find a CD containing Virgin Net on the inside back cover of this book. Before installing Virgin Net, please shut down any other applications on your computer.

Windows 95 users: Insert the CD and follow the on-screen instructions.

Windows 3.1 users: Insert the CD and and select File from the top menu, then choose Run. Type: d:\virgin.net\win31\setup31.exe and follow the on-screen instructions.

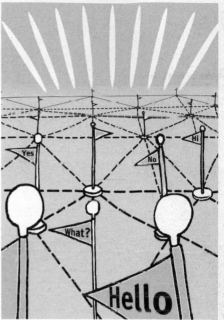

Illustrations: Matt Carless

2. Register

After installation comes registration. Remember to check that your computer, modem and telephone line are all linked up and that the modem is switched on. Just follow the on-screen instructions to get your unique Virgin Net Username and Password. Please note them down for future reference. You will be asked for personal and payment details. This information is to set up your account and payments will only begin if you remain with us once your free trial period has expired.

3. Connect

To go online, turn on your modem and computer and double-click the Virgin Net icon on your Windows 95 desktop. If you are using Windows 3.1, double-click the Virgin Net icon in the Virgin Net program group.

Wherever you are in the UK, you will be connected through a local rate phone call. Remember, however, that your Virgin Net subscription does not include the price of this call, the charges will appear on your next phone bill.

Rave reviews for Virgin Net

"Internet Access Provider of the Year"
UK Internet Awards, '97

"This Internet Service Provider calls the shots"
The Independent, November '96

"Simplicity itself"
Ideal Home, December '96

"Excellent for price and service"
PC Answers, July '97

"Virgin Net wins on good value, excellent software
and top technical support"
*Winner of Internet Service Provider of the Year,
Internet Magazine, '97*

"Richard Branson's crew have taken the market by storm with keen
prices and top quality support"
PC Answers, July '97

"Easy to use and good value"
*Rated best value Internet Service Provider –
Which? Consumer Guide, June '97*